GOLF FORE EVER

GOLF FORE EVER

GUIDE FOR BEGINNING GOLFERS

MIKEDEAGLE

"Your story is our priority"

LitPrime Solutions
21250 Hawthorne Blvd
Suite 500, Torrance, CA 90503
www.litprime.com
Phone: 1-800-981-9893

Published by LitPrime Solutions   07/13/2023

ISBN: 979-8-88703-265-8(sc)
ISBN: 979-8-88703-266-5(e)

Library of Congress Control Number: 2023912629

Any people depicted in stock imagery provided by iStock are models, and such images are being used for illustrative purposes only.

Certain stock imagery © iStock.

Because of the dynamic nature of the Internet, any web addresses or links contained in this book may have changed since publication and may no longer be valid. The views expressed in this work are solely those of the author and do not necessarily reflect the views of the publisher, and the publisher hereby disclaims any responsibility for them.

CONTENTS

PART 3: PLANNING A GOLF TRIP

PART 4: GOLF ON A BET–THE HOLE IN ONE AND FUN GAMES TO MAKE GOLF A LITTLE MORE INTERESTING

PART 5: THE CHAMPIONS OF GOLF AND GOLF'S MOST PRESTIGIOUS TOURNAMENTS

PART 6: GOLF'S CHAMPIONS AND GOLF TERMINOLOGY–A MUST FOR THE BEGINNING GOLFER

ACKNOWLEDGMENTS

I would like to dedicate this book to my father, Michael Sr., and to my aunt and godmother, Andrianna, who both left this world much too soon. My sincere and deep appreciation to my sister Lu Anne and my mother Antoinette, without whose encouragement and inspiration I may not have had the fortitude and determination to complete this guide, which I started almost twelve years ago. I would also like to offer my thanks to my nephews, James and Christopher Hopkins, who assisted with the photo illustrations included in the guide, and to Cathi and my son Tommy, who helped with formatting and editing throughout the writing process. Thank you to all family members for their support and assistance in the creation of this guide for beginning golfers.

I have one additional person to acknowledge as he played a crucial role in the editing of this Golf Guide for Beginners. He was my consultant during the final editorial process, and he went above and beyond any of my expectations to ensure our best chances for success. I thank you, George Nedeff, and I sincerely hope to work with you on future projects.

ABOUT THE AUTHOR

Before we commence on our journey into the wonderful world of *Golf Fore Ever*, I would like to provide you with some additional insight as to what prompted me to create this golf guide for beginners.

I grew up in the Canarsie section of Brooklyn, New York, and was first introduced to golf when I was twenty-one years old. Although I hate to admit it, that was a bit over thirty-five years ago. At that time I was an avid baseball, football, and softball fan, and played all three sports with some level of skill. Golf was not as popular in the sixties and seventies as it is now, thanks in a large part to the arrival of Tiger Woods on the scene. So other sports took precedence. I enjoyed these sports so much that at one time I played on as many as four softball teams simultaneously. During one of the games circa 1979, on an adjacent field to McDonald Avenue, near Avenue S in Brooklyn, New York, I tore my hamstring pretty severely while attempting to beat out an infield grounder while running to first base. Although I was safe, my competitive softball days were over. It was a painful experience, to say the least, and my hamstring did not heal very well. I rested it for the balance of the season only to reinjure it in the second game I played in the very next season. Subsequent to the injury I still played for fun, but it was not the same as vying for the batting title in the Flatbush League in Brooklyn or being part of a team competing to win the championship of the league. With my competitive softball, football, and baseball days behind me, a new chapter was about to open for me in sports. As I mentioned earlier, my father's friend introduced me to golf when I was twenty-one years old. One day my buddy and I were tossing the football around in his yard and his dad asked us if we would like to join him at the golf range. We both looked at each other tentatively, but we agreed to go and check out what the golf buzz was all about. This was the era when Jack Nicklaus, Tom Watson, Gary Player, Lee Trevino, and Arnold Palmer were going head-to-head week after week at golf tournaments and especially at the majors, like the Masters and the

U.S. Open. When we arrived at the range we had to rent clubs since we had never played golf and did not have any equipment of our own. My friend's father had some basic knowledge of the game and gave us some tips on how to hold the club and address the ball. Now, I was ready and I said to myself, "How hard can it be to hit an object that's standing still?" I approached the tee, placed the ball, and quickly found out after my first swing attempt that it surely was not as easy as it appeared. It was one thing to make contact with the ball, which was difficult enough, but another to hit the ball straight ahead. After hitting—or should I say attempting to hit—about forty or fifty golf balls, my friend and I realized that golf was going to be more challenging than we originally had anticipated. The challenge is one of the things that intrigued me about golf from the outset. Another thing I realized is that contrary to popular belief at that time, golf required a certain degree of athleticism if one were to attain any level of skill at the sport. The hand–eye coordination required to strike the ball well was every bit as challenging as hitting a baseball traveling at ninety- plus miles an hour in your direction.

I always enjoyed a challenge, and golf certainly provided that. Over the next few years I went back to the range and also played golf a number of times with my friends. I liked the game, but since I was so involved with other sports I did not have the time to pursue golf also. The hamstring injury may have been a blessing in disguise. If not for that injury I may never have taken up a sport that I would become more passionate about than I could have imagined. I remembered how enjoyable and challenging the experience was, and I figured it was now the time to get serious about learning to play. I emphasize learning because there is much more to golf than beating a little white ball around the golf course. Once I started playing I became enamored with golf immediately, and the rest is history. I've been playing and enjoying the game of golf for over thirty years now and have never looked back.

The main reason I decided to create this manual is to provide some helpful information to the novice or newcomer to the sport that I wish I had available to me when I first started playing golf. I sincerely hope that the information provided in the following chapters will make golf an even more enjoyable and rewarding experience for you than it was for me and help you avoid the pitfalls I encountered when first learning to play. Enjoy!

"FORE" WORD

G olf Fore Ever offers advice and information on learning to play golf the "right way." This information is derived from the author's thirty-plus-year journey of learning and playing this incredible game. From his very first experience on the golf course, he recognized his passion for the sport. This guide will help the new golfer to avoid the pitfalls and some of the more common beginner mistakes, like overspending on your first set of golf clubs, not learning to play properly before venturing out onto the golf course, and proper golf etiquette, an important but often overlooked fundamental of the game. His advice will include information on the steps to preparing and executing a proper golf swing, including the grip and setup.

Readers also will find within the pages of this book a brief history of the author's timeline as a golfer, including tips and advice for beginning and seasoned golfers alike. *Golf Fore Ever* provides a variety of information that touches on every imaginable aspect of golf and also encompasses the steps for curing the dreaded slice. He will also address how to adjust for wind and uneven terrain on the golf course. The reader will also find highlights and recommendations on some of the nation's greatest golf courses and resorts, such as Disney World and Myrtle Beach, known as the golf capital of the world.

His emphasis on proper golf etiquette isn't found in many other books on golf. His advice is derived from his own encounters, victories, and failures, and is not a book backed by no experience or depth.

He would like to wish a warm welcome to the beginning and seasoned golfer alike and heartily extend to them his signature phrase, "Happy golfing to all!"

PART 1:

START PLAYING GOLF: THE BASICS

CHAPTER 1

LEARN TO PLAY GOLF
THE RIGHT WAY

One of the reasons I decided to create this guide is to help the new golfer get started the "right way," as there is much more to golf than meets the eye. When I started playing golf some thirty-plus years ago, I was lucky enough to have a few friends who had older brothers or dads who played and were willing to take us out with them. So I learned most of the rules of golf and golf etiquette from the outset. Etiquette is described in the dictionary as "a special code of behavior or courtesy." A true golfer who follows the rules and wants to play the game of golf properly, or the "right way," will adhere to this special code of behavior and extend the many courtesies associated with golf to his fellow players. These are the written, unwritten, and all-too-often-overlooked rules of golf that will be elaborated on in another chapter.

In my opinion, there are four things necessary to get started playing golf: First, you must have a desire to learn. Second, you will need golf equipment. Third, you as a new golfer should have some basic knowledge of how to swing a club and the rules of golf. And fourth, make sure you know your golf etiquette. As you will note, I emphasize the etiquette aspect of golf. As you become a more experienced player, it will become more apparent to you as to why.

The first of four necessities to play golf is a desire to learn, which is an obvious one and does not require addressing at this time. The second requirement noted is equipment, which will be discussed in this chapter.

Equipment

In order to play most sports, you require proper equipment. Golf equipment can vary drastically in price, and it is not necessary to purchase expensive equipment when first learning to play. Professional golfers have their equipment altered to their personal specifications and height requirements. Since golf is their livelihood, they want to play their best so that they have a better opportunity to earn the maximum amount possible. In golf, the slightest inconsistency in a player's equipment can drastically affect the outcome of the shot played. The length, weight, and loft of each club are adjusted to maximize the results that a professional golfer can attain with each club. Investing in a custom set of golf clubs can be fairly expensive but may be worth the investment if you enjoy golf and want to play your best.

(**FORE Advice:** If you really enjoy golf and want to get serious about playing and scoring well, I would recommend investing in a custom set of clubs. It will provide you with a distinct advantage over the off-the-rack clubs.)

There are a number of ways to acquire your first set of golf clubs and the accessories to go with them. Since golf clubs can vary in price from $150 to over $2,000 per set for the newest high-tech equipment, you have to be careful not to overspend on your first set of golf clubs. As you gain experience playing golf, you will learn the subtleties and varied results you can attain with different clubs. When you find a club you feel comfortable with, you may also find that it will help your ball-striking ability. PING is actually the only manufacturer of clubs I know of who offers an innovative color-coded set to match the varied heights of different golfers. When you become a more experienced player and are ready to purchase a new set of golf clubs, PING provides an option that could save you some money. You may want to explore PING as a potential choice of clubs in which to invest. You can purchase a set of PING irons and save on the fee for the time it would take a golf professional to fit you for a custom set of clubs, which could be substantial.

The standard rack set of clubs is manufactured for men and women of average height, but as you know all of us are not average in height or stature. The off-the-rack set will work for most individuals who are plus or minus up to three inches from the average height, say five-nine for men and five-four for women. Once you exceed that margin, the effectiveness of your ball striking becomes proportionately lessened with the degree of variance from the height of the average person.

It is most important to acquire some type of equipment initially and see if you enjoy the game before making any substantial investments. If budget is an issue, and you are still on the fence about whether you will enjoy golf, check with family members, such as your father, mother, sister, brother, aunt, or uncle. If any of them has ever played golf, there is a good chance they may have an old or extra set of clubs laying around that they could give or lend you. This option will allow you to save some money while determining whether you enjoy golf. Another economical method of acquiring clubs is to check out garage sales in the neighborhood. You may be surprised to see what people are looking to get rid of and at real bargain prices. Also the Internet offers a huge selection of clubs at very good prices, but you should check with someone knowledgeable about golf and golf clubs before making any online purchases.

If none of these options are available to you, then I would recommend visiting your local golf or sporting goods store, such as Dick's, Golfsmith, Modell's, Wal-Mart, or whatever sporting goods stores that may be in your area. They usually carry starter sets for the beginner, and you may even be able to pick up a used set of PINGs, Taylor Made, Callaway, or another premium brand of club at a really good price. The golf employees who work at Dick's and Golfsmith are usually able to offer more professional assistance. If you are serious about golf and ready to purchase, then ask for the most knowledgeable staff member or golf professional to assist with selecting the right set of golf clubs for you.

Another option is to go to your local golf course and ask for the teaching professional. Explain to them that you have a desire to learn to play golf and see if they offer a special rate on a golf lesson or a series of lessons for the beginner. Make sure to stress that you are a beginner, because some professional instructors assume that their pupils have more knowledge about golf than they do when they commence with their lessons. Don't be afraid to let them know you have not played before and need someone to start with the very basics of golf instruction. Once they have observed the characteristics of your swing and noted your height and stature, they will be better able to advise you on what type of clubs will be best suited for your swing and ability.

The beginning golfer does not need to carry a full set of fourteen clubs, which is the maximum number of clubs allowed by the rules of golf. Many of the starter sets normally include a driver, and a 3- or 5-wood, a 5-iron, a 7-iron, a 9-iron, a pitching or sand wedge, and a putter. You will also need a golf bag for your clubs, which is usually included with the starter sets. Besides golf clubs and a bag, some of the other items you will need are the following:

- golf balls—(**FORE Advice:** I would recommend purchasing about two dozen of the more economically priced balls, such as Maxfli, Pinnacle, Top Flite, Noodle, or Slazenger. Beginning golfers will have a tendency to lose more golf balls when they play golf. It won't hurt the pocketbook so much when it costs a dollar per ball, as opposed to four dollars each, which some of the more expensive balls—like Titleist Pro V and Pro V1x—go for.)

- (**FORE Info:** A few years ago, golf balls were manufactured with various compression ratings: 80, 90, and 100. The amount of distance and performance derived from the different- compression balls is determined by the player's swing speed and how much the ball compresses when the club makes contact with the ball. Golf professionals would most likely use a 100, or at minimum a 90 compression ball. Their swing speed and mechanics allow them to attain the maximum compression to achieve optimum performance and distance utilizing the higher compression ball. Due to the innovative manufacturing capabilities and technology of the golf ball companies of today, the compression rating is no longer an issue. The new golf balls are now constructed to allow the golfer to achieve the greatest distance, height and overall performance in their drives, approach shots from the fairway, and touch around the greens. The different performance criteria will guide you in selecting a golf ball that's right for your game.

When I first learned to play I used a golf bag I borrowed, a driver, a 3-wood, a 5-wood, a 5-iron, a 7-iron, a 9-iron, a sand wedge, and a putter. They were more than enough clubs to play with and enjoy the game. The different-numbered clubs are used for varied distances. For example, the driver is the least lofted club, which means you can achieve the maximum distance utilizing this club. The subsequent clubs noted—3-wood, 5-wood, 5-, 7-, and 9-iron, and sand wedge—all have increasing angles of loft. As the number increases on the club, the resulting distance decreases accordingly. Each number increase will progressively represent a decrease in distance of approximately ten to twenty yards, depending on your ability and if you are using a wood or iron.

(FORE Advice: A good way to gauge the different distances you can attain with each club is to spend some time on the golf range after you have learned the proper fundamentals of the golf swing.)

Let's get back to equipment. Some other pieces of equipment I would strongly recommend purchasing are:

- golf towel—This will be used to wipe dirt off the club after it makes contact with the ground

- golf shoes—Although not absolutely necessary, they will greatly assist with stability as you swing the golf club.
- golf tees (**FORE Advice:** There are different golf tee lengths made for different drivers, woods, and irons. I recommend that you pick up an assortment of varied length tees, 2 1/8" long for woods and irons, and 2 ¾" or 3 ¼" for drivers, depending on the make, model, and size of the driver. If you are not sure what types of tees to purchase, check with your golf professional or a salesperson for recommendations of which size tee would be compatible with your golf equipment.)
- golf glove—Not mandatory or required. A glove will give you a distinct advantage in gripping and holding the club more effectively.
- ball markers—The markers are used on the green to mark your ball so that you will not block the path of another player. This is also a rule of golf etiquette.
- divot repair tool—Used to repair the indentation made in the green when the golf ball lands. This is a rule of golf etiquette to be addressed in a subsequent chapter. (**FORE Advice:** Although not required to play golf, you may want to consider packing the following ancillary items: Band-Aids, sunscreen, and insect repellent. You never know when you might need them, and it's better to be prepared to allow for maximum comfort while you play.)

Summary

Here are the options for acquiring golf clubs and equipment:

1. Borrow from a relative or friend.
2. Check out garage sales.
3. Make an online purchase (**FORE Advice:** Check with someone knowledgeable before making an online purchase.)

4. Visit your local sporting goods store and look for starter or used sets. (**FORE Advice:** Ask for assistance from a golf pro when the option is available.)

5. Consult with a golf professional at your local golf course, driving range, or country club.

6. Since there are so many manufacturers of golf clubs, I have listed a few of the better known and more popular brands:

7. PING—I listed it first because, as noted previously, it is the only manufacturer of golf clubs that makes color-coded sets for the different height requirements of a golfer.

8. TaylorMade—a widely used brand by many of the top professional golfers.

9. Callaway—another top name and used by Phil Mickelson.

10. Nike—Tiger Woods's sponsor and club provider.

11. Titleist—a well-known and very popular manufacturer of golf balls that also produces a high quality golf club line.

12. Mizuno—also a high-end golf club manufacturer.

13. Cobra

14. Cleveland

15. MacGregor

16. Wilson

If you decide to purchase golf clubs by any of the manufacturers listed above, they will provide you with the necessary equipment to play golf as long as you have prepared properly to play.

(**FORE Warning:** The results achieved using any brand of golf clubs will only be as good as the skill level of the person using them.)

Instruction

There are a number of ways to learn how to play golf. At the time I started playing golf, which was over thirty years ago, I opted to teach myself. I read *The Golfers Bible and Ben Hogan's Five Lessons: The Modern Fundamentals of Golf.* Both books were very informative and contained valuable information to help a new golfer start to play. In my opinion—and anyone who knows about the history of golf would agree—Ben Hogan was one of the most naturally skilled golfers who ever played the game. I was confident that any book on golf that he authored could only be informative and benefit someone who wanted to learn how to play. I can attest firsthand that it helped me tremendously. When I first started to play golf there were not as many golf professionals available to teach the average golfer. In retrospect, depending on one's budget and how quickly one wants to develop his golf skills, I would recommend lessons from a teaching professional. Unless you are born with a natural talent for the sport—from my experience those so gifted are few and far between—lessons are the way to go. There are many options for taking golf lessons, and the most important thing you can do is select an instructor or teaching professional who specializes in teaching the beginning golfer. Many teachers might be skilled golfers and good instructors for the seasoned golfer, but some do not know how to impart their knowledge to the beginner. I would suggest getting a recommendation from someone who plays, if possible, or interviewing the prospective golf professional, explaining that you are a new golfer, and seeing if you can get a feel for whether they would be right for you. I am self-taught and have been playing golf for over thirty years. The learning curve is different for everyone, but I've noticed that most golfers who are good at other sports, especially baseball and hockey, have a tendency to play golf well. Having been self-taught, I had to experiment with different techniques over the years to improve my game. To this day I am continuously reading up on the latest and greatest advancements on instruction and golf equipment and experimenting with various techniques to try to improve my golfing skills. With the increased popularity of golf, thanks in part to the arrival of Tiger Woods on the scene, the teaching techniques and availability of teaching professionals has increased tremendously. I feel strongly that lessons are the best option, if cost is not an obstacle. Golf is a sport that requires muscle memory for a repetitive swing. Once your swing techniques and mechanics are ingrained in the subconscious, it will be harder to correct if you do not learn properly at the outset. Having the proper basics is crucial for learning to play the right way. Golf will be so much more enjoyable if you play well and learn the proper techniques for the swing. I actually took a lesson a few years after I started playing golf but I was very disappointed with the teaching pro. All the lesson consisted of was him watching me swing and saying, "Okay, that looks good." He offered no recommendations on grip, setup, tempo, swing path, repetitive swing thoughts, grip pressure, backswing, follow-through, etc.—basically all of the most important fundamentals of the golf swing. Because of that experience, I was soured on lessons for quite some time until I saw some good teaching professionals in action with other students. So don't let an isolated experience that I once had dissuade you from taking golf lessons. There are a number of steps you must take to master the correct golf swing, and a teaching professional will be able to show you each of them. You will learn much quicker than reading about them and experimenting for years like I did. Seven fundamental steps to a good golf swing are:

- the grip—how you set the club in your hands.
- the setup—how you address the ball and the positioning of your body and alignment in relation to the ball.
- the waggle—a trigger or initial movement to allow the swing to start properly.
- tempo—the rate of speed from the start of the backswing through the hitting area and the follow-through.
- the backswing—the move immediately following the waggle, the cocking of the wrist, and the turning or coiling of the body together with the arms and shoulders away from the target to prepare for the downswing.
- the downswing—immediately follows the backswing and is the part of the swing where impact with the ball takes place, including the pronation of the hands as they pass through the contact point with the golf ball.
- the follow-through—the completion of the golf swing, which concludes the transfer of your weight from your

right side to your left, and your body is positioned to face the target.

(**FORE Reference:** This is for right-handed golfers, and the opposite would be true for lefties.) If any of the aforementioned steps are not executed properly, your shot can be greatly affected. With the advent of video instruction, the instructor can play back the video and show you exactly what you were doing right or wrong during the course of each step of your swing. You've heard the expression that "a picture is worth a thousand words." Well, it would most definitely apply in this case. Although you can read a book on golf or watch instructional videos (and some are very good), it is still not the same as being taught firsthand by a good golf professional.

(**FORE Reference:** You can find a list of the top teaching professionals in the country in the *Golf Digest* magazines, or visit their Web site at <u>www.</u> golfdigest.com.) Although I am self-taught and for the most part an above- average player, I often wonder how much better I could have been and how much faster I could have progressed had I invested initially in professional instruction. One of the main reasons I decided to write this guide is to provide as much information as possible about the pitfalls I encountered while learning to play golf. I want to offer some insight and guidance, from someone who has faced many of the aforementioned pitfalls and the wonderful experiences of golf, on how to overcome and enjoy them all respectively. Let me clarify what I mean by pitfalls because it makes it sound like golf can be problematic, and in reality with golf there are no real pitfalls to speak of. Some of the pitfalls I am referring to are:

- overspending on your first set of clubs
- not taking lessons when you may have had the opportunity
- not adhering to golf course rules and etiquette because you didn't know any better
- not giving golf enough of a chance to learn, play, and enjoy before possibly giving up.

There are so many more positive aspects than negative to be gained from playing golf, and I want to be sure to emphasize that point. Some of the positive points of playing golf that I am referring to are:

- Golf is great exercise, especially if you walk as opposed to taking a motorized golf cart.
- Hitting a bucket or two of golf balls at the range can be a real workout.
- Golf allows you the opportunity to meet some interesting people, as my experience playing golf over the years has shown me.
- Golf can be used as a business tool, as many deals are made on the golf course. You can invite a perspective client to play golf and enjoy a leisurely day with them before they sign on the bottom line.
- Playing golf provides the opportunity to visit some of the most scenic and beautiful resort destinations in the world.
- It will also allow you to enjoy the intrinsic beauty of nature and the animal and plant life that abound on and around most golf courses.
- Most of all, you might learn a lot about the game of life itself through your experience with this unusually challenging sport.

With golf it's just you against the golf course. I think that is enough said for now. You will enjoy learning the rest of the benefits of golf for yourself, as they are a wonderful and integral part of the journey while learning to play. Golf can be fun no matter how skilled a player may be, but it is human nature to enjoy a sport more if you play well or excel at it. Wouldn't you agree? I can attest from personal experience that if I score in the seventies or low eighties in a golf round, I feel much more exhilarated than if I shoot in the high eighties or above. Taking lessons with the right teaching professional will help you attain a higher skill level much faster than self-teaching, and it will allow you to enjoy the game that much more. Do not be discouraged if your initial score is well over 100. The average golfer probably scores in the mid to high nineties if he is being honest and counting all the strokes that the United States Golf Association (USGA) rules dictate. Don't be disheartened or decide to quit if your score is not what you expect at the beginning. It took me a number of months before I could break 100, and a year or so to play well enough to join a golf league, which is pretty typical for most new golfers.

Golf lessons for the beginner can range in cost from approximately $45 for a thirty- or forty-five–minute session to $150, depending on the credentials of the golf professional, and around $650 to $700, plus or minus, for a series of about ten lessons. Depending on a person's budget, a series of ten to twenty lessons is a good start for the beginner and will be well worth the investment. Again, this depends on the experience and ability of the instructor and how fast you can learn. If you can only afford one to three lessons, it is better than none, and at least you can receive the basic information regarding the grip, setup, and swing to get you started in the right direction.

If you opt for lessons, then it will probably take ten to twenty sessions for you to obtain some level of proficiency in most fundamentals of the golf swing. The sessions can be scheduled weekly, biweekly, or daily, depending on the availability of you and the instructor. At the end of your series of lessons, and also during the sessions, the instructor will give you exercises and practice drills to help you incorporate the proper swing techniques into your daily routine.

(**FORE Advice:** Make sure to practice the drills and golf exercises your instructor may assign for you. It will allow you to progress much faster and make the lessons more worthwhile.) Do not get discouraged if you do not grasp all of the information immediately because each golfer will learn and progress at his own pace. If you are having problems subsequent to your lessons, you may need a follow-up lesson periodically to fine-tune your game.

There are also golf schools that offer one- to five-day packages, whereby you can plan a relaxing vacation at a beautiful resort and learn to play golf at the same time. This method would probably be the most expedient and proficient way to learn to play but also the most costly. If money is no object, then I highly recommend golf school (or minimally golf lessons). In golf school you will receive instruction on successive days and your instructors can monitor your swing faults and make corrective suggestions in a timely manner. This will keep any faults from becoming bad habits that could impede your learning progress because they will be addressed and corrected almost immediately. They will also advise you on what you are doing right and give you practice drills to help with muscle memory and a proper repetitive swing.

If you are on a tight budget you can still opt to self-teach, like I did, or maybe request a lesson or two as a holiday gift. Another option is to ask a friend or relative who plays golf to teach you the basic rules, swing fundamentals, and golf etiquette. I will elaborate on golf etiquette, a very important but often overlooked fundamental of the game, in the next section.

I visited the local Golfsmith store about two years ago, and I noticed they had an area within the store just for golf lessons and also another area for practice. I was a bit disenchanted with my game at the time and I wondered if they might be able to help get my swing back on track. The lesson section was called GolfTEC, and I went over and introduced myself to one of the teaching professionals there. After we spoke, I was convinced that he could help me with my golf game, so I bit the bullet and signed up for a series of lessons for about $700. This included ten lessons with one-on-one instruction, including hookup to a video monitor and swing analyzing device, whereby he could play back and show me my golf swing in action. He was able to point out my swing problems and deficiencies almost immediately and offered me some swing exercises to help get my game back on track. It seemed like a lot of money at the time, but it was well worth the investment to be able to play better and enjoy golf so much more in such a short amount of time. Golfers are unable to view their swing; even if they could, it is very difficult to analyze a golf swing and make the proper adjustments to correct one's faults, especially for the beginner. This is why I highly recommend lessons for the new golfer with virtually no experience. Even the most seasoned golf professionals, like Tiger

Woods, Phil Mickelson, Fred Couples, Jim Furyk, and many of their peers, rely on lessons with a good teaching professional.

The golf pro can recognize a swing fault and help correct the problem more easily than golfers can do themselves, and they are smart enough to realize that. The top three teaching pros in the country are:

- Butch Harmon, formerly Tiger's swing coach and now Phil Mickelson's
- Hank Haney, a great guy and a real gentleman who I once met in Philadelphia at a business seminar and who was formerly Tiger Woods' swing coach.
- David Leadbetter, who is based in Florida at Champions Gate, and another top-notch teaching pro.

The lessons with any of these guys are virtually cost-prohibitive, but their golf academies have many fine professional instructors and offer much more reasonable and affordable rates.

Between lessons you may want to keep up with the latest and greatest in golf equipment, golf tips, golf instruction, golf tournament results, golf vacation destinations, and other enjoyable and interesting information on golf. In order to keep current with the latest and greatest in golf, I recommend a subscription to one or more of the available golf magazines. I subscribe to *Golf Digest*, which in my opinion is the best and most informative golf magazine available. *Golf World*, a sister magazine to *Golf Digest*, offers weekly results on all the professional tours and more informative golf articles, including golf travel destinations, clothing trends, and new equipment. Another good golf magazine that I recommend is appropriately titled *Golf* and is also recognized as one of the top-rated publications on the sport. Many professional golfers, like Jack Nicklaus, Tiger Woods, Phil Mickelson, Tom Watson, Ernie Els, and others, are on the staff of these magazines and offer many of the tips and swing techniques to the reader that made them the best players in the world. The newsstand price is roughly four times the cost of a subscription, so I highly recommend you subscribe to at least one magazine to save some money and enjoy the game that much more.

If you decide to subscribe to only one magazine, then I suggest *Golf Digest*. It offers the most information for a very reasonable price. The subscription can range from $12 to $19.95 annually, depending on if, where, and when you see an advertisement or special offer. I wish you all much success in the learning process, and I hope whatever option you choose allows you to enjoy the journey as much I did. Happy golfing to all!

Golf Etiquette

Since the beginning of this golf guide, I have been emphasizing the importance of golf etiquette. I would like you to read the following post I wrote in my golf blog in January 2008.

> Golf Etiquette—An important Part
> of a Gentleperson's Game

> There was a time not so long ago that I may have used "Gentleman's" in the title, as opposed to "Gentleperson's," but then the ladies would have been all over me and not in a good way. The game of golf did, however, originate as a gentleman's game. Have you ever wondered about where the term "golf" originated? When I was in high school, not all that many years ago, my history teacher, who was a really cool guy, used to digress in class from time to time. One day we arrived on the subject of golf and he began a dissertation on it. One of the things he explained was the derivation of the word "GOLF." Supposedly, it was a term created by a bunch of gentlemen, and I use the term loosely, who at the time would have been considered chauvinistic to say the least, most especially by today's standards. He explained that the **G** stood for GENTLEMEN, **O** stood for ONLY, **L** stood for LADIES, and **F** stood for FORBIDDEN, so together it read, "Gentlemen Only

Ladies Forbidden." I cannot attest for sure if this was the actual derivation of the word, but it makes for an interesting, if not controversial, topic to say the least. I guess the men of that era were looking for a little alone time with the guys. My personal opinion is that men and women should both have their space but it should be more of a mutual thing and not a mandatory edict.

I may have digressed a bit there myself, so back to golf etiquette. What is etiquette? Etiquette is described in the dictionary as "any special code of behavior or courtesy." Golf is a game based on special codes of behavior and courtesies where this would especially come into play. One of the first rules of golf etiquette, and a very important one, is to learn to play properly before going out on the golf course. I've been playing golf for about thirty years or so and there are many golfers, especially beginning golfers, who venture out on the course without a clue as to how to play, the basic rules of golf, and the etiquette required by the game.

The tee times on the golf courses of today are set up approximately eight to twelve minutes apart. Depending on how busy the course may be and whether it's a local municipal course, a resort course, or a country club, the pace of play is expected to be maintained at a certain rate. Speaking from an experienced golfer's point of view—and you will be there one day—it is not fun to wait extensively for your next shot while the group in front of you is taking as many strokes as possible to get the ball near or into the hole. The rule of thumb of about fifteen minutes a hole is a good gauge for all golfers, and you should try your best to keep up with that rate of play. This means that the eighteen holes would be played in about four and a half hours. When I first learned to play golf—and I subsequently taught my significant other to abide by the same courtesies—I was told to take a swing or two. If I was not proficient enough to achieve a certain distance or maybe even miss the ball completely, then I was courteous to my fellow players and didn't take an inordinate number of strokes just for the sake of swinging the club. It is not only discourteous to your fellow players, but the improper swing will become ingrained into your subconscious, making it more difficult to correct in the future. In order to maintain the pace of play and observe etiquette, pick your ball up, place it at a spot near the rest of your group, and try again. It is no great accomplishment to attain a total of 20 on a golf hole just for the sake of keeping score. You should repeat this process until you reach the green, at which time you would putt to the hole. The same principle would hold true on the green. If you attempt to putt a number of times and can't seem to sink the ball in the cup, then pick it up and go on to the next hole. Most of us have been there, so it's only a matter of time before you get the hang of it. Try to play with people who have golf experience, especially for your first few times out, and ask them to teach you the rules and etiquette associated with the game. If you have decided to take lessons, which I highly recommend, then ask your instructor to advise you on the basic rules and etiquette of golf. Also, schedule a tee time when the course is not so busy. Ask the starter at the golf course, or whoever is taking tee times on a particular day, to suggest a time when the golf course is not too crowded so that you will feel more relaxed and less pressured with less people around.

Some of the rules of golf etiquette are:

- Learn the basic rules of golf before venturing out on a regulation golf course, and do not break 90 percent of them before finishing the first hole.
- Stand to the side and out of the view of your fellow golfers, remaining still and quiet while they address and hit their ball, especially while on the tee area.
- Repair your divot, which is a mark or indentation made by the golf ball landing on the putting green. It is proper golf etiquette to also repair one or two others.
- Wait patiently off to the side while the player farthest from the hole hits first, and be ready to hit when your turn comes.
- Do not step in one's putting line while on the green. (**FORE Warning:** While it may seem trite, an indentation caused by the player's footprint can throw a putt off line and can

become a serious problem, especially if there is a wager on the line. I'm being facetious, but some players can get pretty testy about anything that can affect their putts and score, especially where money or a match is involved.)

- Do not take an excessive amount of time looking for a lost ball (three to five minutes maximum).

- Concede a short putt, especially for the beginner, so as to keep the pace of play moving. (**FORE Warning:** This is not allowed by the USGA Rules of Golf for professionals or amateurs in competitive play.)

- Be considerate enough to allow a quick playing group behind you to play through.

- Do not take more than twice the number of strokes than noted for par on any given hole, especially for the beginning golfer. (**FORE Warning:** The USGA Rules of Golf require all strokes to be counted until the golf ball is sunk into the cup. The suggestion to keep your total score to double par is for the beginning golfer to help keep the pace of play moving and should not be adhered to after a player has reached a certain level of skill.)

- Repair or replace a fairway divot, which is a clump of grass removed in the fairway by the swing of your club.

- Yell "Fore" out loud if you hit an errant shot that goes off line and anywhere near another group of golfers. (**FORE Warning:** A golf ball can be a dangerous weapon if aimed or directed at another person, so never fool around and aim toward another person because the result could be debilitating or even deadly.)

- Do not drive your cart on or around the green or tee area.

- Adhere to the local rules of the golf course.

- Do not mark your score in the area around the green while another group is waiting to hit up.

- Have the integrity to write your correct score on the card. (**FORE Advice:** It is not critical for the beginner to keep actual score.)

- Return a lost club to the pro shop so that a fellow player can retrieve it after his round.
- Wear proper golf attire while on the course.

Golf is, after all, a gentleperson's game. I think you get the point. There are many more courtesies to be extended to your playing companions and fellow golfers. You will learn them as you gain more experience playing golf. As a new golfer, the importance of etiquette may take a backseat because it is not as exciting as hitting a great shot to a tight pin placement. But, when first learning to play is perhaps the most critical time to adhere to this all-too-often-overlooked aspect of the game. By observing etiquette from the outset it will become second nature to you and will aid you in learning to play the game of golf the right way. Observe these simple courtesies so that you and your fellow golfers will enjoy the journey all the more.

CHAPTER 2

THE GOLF SWING SEVEN-
STEP CHECKLIST

Although I am not actually a golf professional, I have taught myself and a number of other players how to golf—and fairly well at that. I have a good eye for the basics of the golf swing and the technique involved to perform it correctly. It is easier for me to observe another player and offer advice to fix a problematic part of his golf swing than it would be to correct my own swing faults. I will only give advice to someone I know very well or if someone asks me what he may be doing wrong during the course of his golf swing.

I can tell if someone is swaying or picking up the club too fast, or if they are too tense, which in many cases is the cause of a multitude of swing problems. For some, the grip on the club may be too weak or too strong or they are set up too close or too far from the ball. Many beginning golfers reach out with their arms instead of allowing their hands and arms to fall more naturally down into a slot in front of them. I can also tell if they are set up square to their target line, and if there are a number of other swing or setup flaws.

Before we get to the seven steps of the golf swing, I would like to address another overlooked part of the setup routine, which is how to correctly tee the golf ball. Teeing the golf ball seems easy enough, but setting the tee at an improper height can cause a multitude of problems when trying to make good solid contact.

(**FORE Warning:** When the tee is set too high or too low in the ground, it will reduce your chances for a successful shot. If too high, you can sky the ball, causing a loss of distance. If too low, you can mishit or top the ball, causing it to dribble off the tee and, thus, losing a tremendous amount of distance even if the golf swing was performed correctly.)

(**FORE Advice:** The rule of thumb, especially for the driver, is that approximately one-half of the diameter of the golf ball should be above the top of the driver when the ball is teed and the club is laid on the ground next to the tee.)

Setting the tee at the correct height will increase your chances for a successful tee shot.

For the other woods and irons, the top of the tee should be placed a bit lower, maybe a quarter of an inch or so above the ground. This is my personal preference because I feel that this height creates a good angle of impact and the resulting trajectory gives me the desired distance I want with each club used. In any case, the top of the wood should be below the top of the golf ball to help ensure a good impact angle to allow the ball to get into the air more readily.

(**FORE Advice:** I recommend some range time and a number of practice sessions, which can be useful in determining what setting height will work best for you.)

Step 1: The Grip

The grip is Step 1 of the seven-step checklist for the golf swing. After years of practicing, and experimenting with different methods and techniques to prepare for and executing the golf swing, the seven steps to follow are the basics for most golfers. As noted previously, I will only present proven ideas and methodology that work for me. Every golfer is different, and what works for one does not always work for someone else. On the other hand, there are basic principles and techniques that can be gainfully utilized by 95 percent of golfers, and I strongly feel that the steps presented here will work for a majority of the readers of this golf guide. I have taken over thirty years of my experience and experimentation with different techniques and methodologies to present this information to you.

The seven steps of the swing checklist are:

1. The Grip
2. The Setup
3. The Waggle
4. The Backswing
5. Tempo
6. The Downswing
7. The Follow-through.

I placed tempo in the middle because it is an integral part of the entire swing from start to finish and will be explained in Step 5.

Ben Hogan possessed one of the most perfect golf swings imaginable. Feel free to emulate any part of his swing techniques. You will not go wrong. I mentioned Ben Hogan here because, as noted previously, I read his book, *Ben Hogan's Five Lessons: The Modern Fundamentals of Golf*, when first learning to play.

When I first learned to play golf, it required a lot of experimenting and reading golf books and magazines in order to really get a feel for the correct golf swing. The grip is a very important and integral part of the golf swing. There are a number of different types of grip methods.

There is the Vardon grip, named after the great Harry Vardon, one of the premier golfers of the early twentieth century.

The illustration shown below is the Vardon grip and is used by many of the great players in golf.

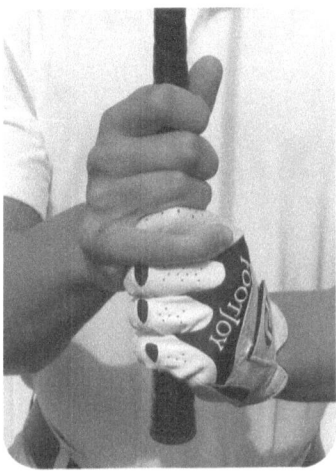

The baseball grip, also appropriately named, is similar to a grip you might use to hold a baseball bat.

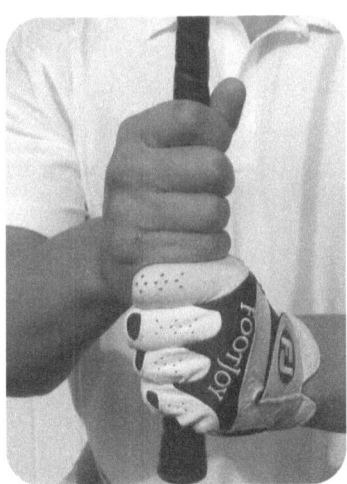

The interlocking grip incorporates the interlocking of the two hands together to form the grip.

The grip, shown above, is an illustration of the interlocking grip and my personal favorite. It is also the preferred grip of Tiger Woods and Jack Nicklaus, the two greatest golfers of all time. (**FORE Advice:** There are many instructional books and DVDs that will illustrate these grips if you would like to see them in a visual presentation.)

If you are sports-oriented and have never read or viewed any instructional information about the grip, then you might have a tendency to use and feel more comfortable with the baseball grip, as I did initially. Although it felt more comfortable, I wasn't satisfied with the results. One day I was playing in a group with a considerably better player who was probably a two- to four-handicap golfer. (**FORE Info:** See Chapter 13 for an explanation of handicap)

I took note of some of his swing techniques, and one of the things that impressed me was as his golf grip. As we were waiting on one hole, I asked him about it. He was utilizing the interlocking grip and he showed me how to do it. I have not changed my grip since. This is how I perform my golf club grip: I set or cradle the club in the creased part of the fingers of my left hand allowing the top of the club to protrude approximately one to one and a half inches past the bottom part of the same hand, which will actually be facing upward and toward your waist and belt area when you set the club to take your grip.

(**FORE Warning:** As you take the grip with the left hand, make sure the clubface stays closed or close to perpendicular to your target line.) Also for a fairly strong grip, which I highly recommend, make sure the first two (or even three) knuckles of your left hand are positioned facing up so that you can see them when looking down on your hand and club. The crease between your thumb and index finger of the left hand should be pointing to your right shoulder if done correctly. Then allow the thumb of the left hand to lie across the top of the grip on a slight angle to the right while keeping the thumb straight and on top of the club. (**FORE Info:** There are a variety of ways to hold the club to create stronger and weaker grips, to allow your swing to work the ball right or left, but a more advanced technique should not be attempted until your game has progressed to a certain level.)

Next, set the club in the creased part of the fingers of the right hand and interlock the pinky of your right hand with the index finger of your left—thus, the derivation of the name "interlocking grip." The meaty part of the palm of your right hand, connected to the thumb, should be facing upward so that you can also see it, similar to the knuckles of the left. And again the crease between the thumb and index finger should be pointing toward your right shoulder. (**FORE Advice:** You can experiment at the range with the adjustment of the strength of the grip and find out what works best for you.)

Turn your hands to the right for a stronger grip and to the left for a weaker grip. Also, please note that the grip methodology noted above is for the right-handed player and should be reversed for the left- handed golfer. Another important thing to remember, which will also be addressed in Step 2: The Setup, is to not let your right shoulder come forward when taking the grip with the right hand. It should remain back and aligned with your left shoulder. It should also be slightly lower than your left since your right hand is set lower on the club when taking the grip.

(**FORE Advice:** To help with your alignment to the target, pick an intermediate target in close proximity in front of you. It could be a leaf, a dandelion, a discoloration in the grass, a pebble, etc. Make sure that the intermediate target is also in line with the golf ball and the intended landing area in the fairway or the green, and use that spot to line up your shot.)

The Vardon grip is similar to the interlocking grip except for the fact that the right pinky finger is cradled between the outside part of the left index and middle finger and does not interlock at all. The baseball grip is basically the same as if you were holding a bat in your hand and preparing to hit a baseball. It is probably the most comfortable, especially to the new golfer, but in my opinion the least effective of the grip selections available. The interlocking or Vardon grips might feel more uncomfortable at first, but once you get used to them you will be much more at ease with the improvement they promote in your game. This is the first part of the swing checklist, and an important one at that. When you are at the range or swinging in your yard, take the time to work on your grip so that it becomes second nature to you.

(**FORE Advice:** I would like to add one very important and often overlooked part of the golf swing. Be sure to relax. Do not let tension creep into any part of your swing, especially your grip. The club should be cradled gently in your hands with about as much pressure as if you were holding a baby's hand or a small bird in your hand, an analogy used by Sam Snead, one of the all-time golfing greats. Make use of the old expression, to let the club do the work. You will be amazed at how swing speed and technique, together with a tension-free body and mind, produce so much greater results.)

Step 2: The Setup

To quote a line from Ed Norton, "Step up, plant your feet firmly, and address the ball—Hello Ball." For all of you *Honeymooner* fans out there, I'm sure you will recall that this was Ed's instruction to Ralph in the famous *Honeymooner* golf episode, which is one of my all-time favorites. In order to prepare for the golf swing, the setup is where you will step up to the ball, place your feet in position, and address the ball. So Ed was pretty accurate in his direction to Ralph, except of course for the "Hello Ball" part.

After the ball is set on the tee, step back and relax. (**FORE Warning:** Make sure to tee the golf ball correctly. Refer to the beginning section of this chapter for information on teeing the golf ball.) The next step is to position your body in relation to the ball. The proper alignment to the target is the key to accuracy in the setup. As noted in a tip in Step 1 of the seven-step checklist, you should choose an intermediate target directly in front of you and in line with the golf ball and your intended landing area. Once you have selected your spot, the next step is to take your stance parallel to that line. (**FORE Advice:** In order to practice aligning correctly to the target, two clubs can be placed on the ground. One will be placed next to the golf ball and will be pointing directly in line with the ball, your intermediate spot and the landing or target area. The other will be placed in parallel to the first but at the area where your feet will be placed. Once you practice for a while utilizing this method, you should acquire a feel for the correct alignment technique.)

Set Up – Aligning to Target

Side View Alignment Front View Alignment

(**FORE Info:** The setup can be performed with the feet and body positioned open or closed—in other words, out of alignment to the target line—which will allow the golfer to work the ball left or right depending on the setup of the golf hole. An open stance will have the right shoulder forward of parallel to the target line, and a closed stance would be the opposite, as the right shoulder will be slightly back of parallel to the target. This setup can be done deliberately to promote the left-to-right or right-to-left ball flight. It is also a technique employed by the more experienced player and is not recommended for the beginning golfer.)

After you have established your line, the next step is the placement of your feet. When I take my stance, I like to place my right foot almost perpendicular or turned slightly to the right of perpendicular to target line, and my left foot is angled about forty-five degrees left of a perpendicular line toward the target. This will allow your upper body to turn more freely and without the restriction of your legs and feet if they were positioned too perpendicular to the target line. (**FORE Warning:** The information provided is meant for the right-handed golfer and should be reversed for those who are left-handed.)

The distance between the feet should be approximately shoulder width, especially for the driver. This allows for stability in the stance, which is important in maintaining good balance throughout the swing. As you take your stance, the knees should be bent slightly and the upper body should be tilted forward a bit at the waist. The head should be kept upright so that the chin does not impede the backswing and shoulder turn, which will be addressed in the next step. As the body tilts slightly forward at the waist and you have taken your grip (as discussed in Step 1), make sure you allow your hands to fall in a relaxed position almost directly below your line of sight if you looked straight down and not too far or too close to your body. I would estimate the hands and club to be approximately six to eight inches away from the body, depending on your height, if done correctly. I will again emphasize the importance of relaxing for the setup and the entire golf swing. I don't mean to the point of falling asleep, but there should be no tension in the body, especially the arms, shoulders, and legs. This will promote a much better tempo and allow the speed of the swing and the club to do the work, which in turn will produce much better results. Since all golfers are different in stature and ability, they may utilize a variation on the ideology noted above. This information and these techniques are derived from personal knowledge and over thirty years of experience playing golf, and I hope it will be helpful to the majority of golfers. There is nothing like practice under the guidance of a golf professional and experience for learning the correct way to swing a golf club. In order for the practice to be efficient and your swing mechanics to improve, you must have the basic foundation in place for the proper swing, playing techniques, and strategies of golf to learn to play the right way.

Step 3: The Waggle

What is a waggle? About thirty-something years ago I may have asked myself that same question. The waggle is a pre-swing move that will help you to trigger the backswing. The key to all phases or steps of the golf swing is to relax. I will keep emphasizing this point because it took me a long time to incorporate the idea into my own swing sequence. I am assuming that the majority of golfers are similar to me in that respect, and it will take a while to get used to. It is a natural tendency to grip the club too tightly and to try to muscle the ball down the fairway to try to achieve the maximum distance possible, or just to show your friends that you can hit the ball farther than they can. But in reality the opposite holds true! Grip the club lighter and tension-free, swing the same way, and voilà you will increase your odds of achieving the results and the distance you desire tenfold. Sorry, another digression. Back to the waggle.

Please note that the waggle is by all means not a necessity to a good or correct golf swing. It is an important option that many golfers employ to help start, or trigger, the backswing. It is a method to promote relaxation and to initiate the swing and correct tempo that will be employed for the entire golf swing. Another method of relaxation before you swing is to take a deep breath and exhale slowly to consciously release any tension. Once you have released the tension, successfully taken your grip, and performed your setup routine as discussed in Step 1 and Step 2, guess what the next step is? The waggle (or any other method you would like to use that works for you—whether it is a deep breath to clear your mind of any interfering thoughts or doing absolutely nothing, if that is your desire).

(**FORE Advice:** The grip and setup should become second nature for you, a routine you should employ for every swing and golf hole that you play.) We have been discussing the waggle for the past few minutes but in actuality, what is it? There are a number of different ways that the waggle can be performed. Don't be afraid to invent and utilize any method that works for you.

As noted earlier, it is a trigger that will promote relaxation and help you to initiate the proper golf swing. The technique that works best for me is to actually rehearse the entire swing. I take my grip, set up to the ball, and actually preview the swing path and moves that I will be performing during my swing. Many times I note that I have taken the club back on an improper swing path or maybe my wrists did not set the club properly. This rehearsal allows me to correct the mistakes prior to my actual swing. Other golfers may just break the wrists off the ball and then return the club to the ball position, or maybe they take a half or three-quarter swing to check if they feel the tempo for the desired swing. You may also choose to rehearse the entire swing, as I do, and any of these techniques are optional. Whatever your waggle method may be, make it part of your swing routine. It may take some experimenting to see what is most comfortable and what works for you, but you will realize the results with practice! Have patience and fun as you learn to play.

Step 4: The Backswing

1. Now that you've taken your grip, performed your setup routine, and rehearsed the waggle, you're ready for action. Before we start the backswing, here are a few reminders:
2. When you tee the golf ball, especially for use with the driver, be sure to set it at the proper height. (FORE Advice: The rule of thumb is that the ball should sit approximately half the diameter of the golf ball above the club head when the club is set on the ground.
3. Stay relaxed during all phases of your swing. (FORE Advice: If you've chosen to incorporate the waggle into your swing routine, then utilize it to its fullest advantage and make it not only your swing trigger but your reminder to relax as well.)
4. Make sure your head is upright so as not to impede the shoulder turn on the backswing.

5. Keep your left arm as straight as possible. (FORE Advice: Keeping the left arm straight may feel uncomfortable at first, but it is critical to promoting consistent ball striking, accuracy, and direction. The left arm will remain straight for right-handed golfers, and the right arm for left-handed golfers.

Now you're ready to go. In the instructional books and videos that I've studied, I have sometimes gotten conflicting information as to how to start the backswing. That does not mean that one method is right or wrong; there are just different techniques and methodology used by different instructors. Immediately after the waggle (or no waggle, if that is your preference), you are ready to execute the swing. When I was first learning to play, most of the instructional material taught a move to start the backswing called the "one-piece takeaway." This means that your two arms, hands, and the club formed a Y shape, which it does, and they would move back away from the target in one piece or motion while maintaining the Y shape.

Illustration of "Y" take away

I had utilized that method for many years before I read about and experimented with the immediate wrist cock, or setting of the wrist right at the onset of the backswing. By this I mean that instead of taking the club back in the Y formation, I would break the wrist and start the backswing in more of an L or V position.

Illustration of "L" or "V" take away

Both methods will work. It is a matter of personal preference and which feels more comfortable for you. In either method the wrists should be set by about waist height and the club should be pointing skyward as your arms approach parallel to the ground.

Your weight should shift to your right side, without a lateral movement of the body, and your upper body should continue turning away from the target with minimal turning of the hips. This will allow a coiling of the upper body and promote a more powerful release as you uncoil and release in your downswing. Make sure your shoulder turns under your chin and your back is facing the target, which will also promote a more powerful and accurate swing.

In Step 2: The Setup, I mentioned tilting the body slightly forward at the waist and remaining in a reasonably upright position. This will create a spine angle that should be maintained during most of your swing. The backswing and the downswing should rotate around the spine as the central pivot point. The more that rotation can be maintained, the more accurate and powerful the results will be.

When you reach the top of the backswing in practice, make sure the club is pointing back toward the target line, which will happen automatically if your wrists are set properly. This will allow the club to stay on line to prepare for the downswing. I would also like to stress again the importance of a straight left arm and relaxing always. Let's recap our checklist so far:

- Tee the ball. This is not on the checklist but I think you may have a problem going forward if you leave this out.
- Take your grip.
- Perform your setup routine and readjust your grip, if necessary.
- Execute the waggle and perform your backswing to prepare for the next step, the downswing.

Step 5: Tempo

We have addressed the grip, the setup, the waggle, and the backswing. Before we proceed any further with the remaining steps to complete the golf swing, I feel this is an important time to discuss tempo. Tempo is not a single part of the swing, but it should be an integral and important part of your entire swing. It is the smooth rhythmic method of timing your pace of swing so that your body works in concert with the club to achieve the most distance, control, and accuracy that your ability will allow. Good tempo will also help promote a consistency in your swing, which in turn will result in consistently better ball striking and, thus, greater scoring capabilities. As in music, tempo is the beat, the speed, and timing whereby your instrument is in sync with the other instruments. Also, as required in music, you have to acquire a feel for the rhythm of your swing. It can be as simple as counting one on the backswing and two for the downswing and follow-through (which will be discussed in Steps 6 and 7) to create the right beat for you. I can tell you from experience that some days my swing tempo is working better than others, and the results on those days can be dramatic. Tempo requires a feel that you must experience before you can really understand the greater potential for a consistently better, more powerful all-around golf swing. An important key to a good golf swing, including good tempo, is relaxation.

A good tempo might be difficult to achieve at first, but it will come with practice. There are some training aids that can help a golfer to learn tempo. One is called Swing Tempo and is endorsed by Hale Irwin and Frank Nobilo, two excellent PGA professionals. In order to find more information about these training aids you can go online to www. swing- tempo.com or call (800) 708-3676. Another tempo trainer is called Swing Speed Radar and can be found at www.swingspeedradar. com. The cost is approximately $130 to $150. If you are having problems achieving that key ingredient in your swing, either one of these devices should help. Make sure to practice this important and integral component of the golf swing for a truly better game. Happy golfing!

Step 6: The Downswing

Now that you've mastered the grip, the setup, the waggle, the backswing, and tempo, the next move should be a piece of cake. In fact, you can let gravity and tempo do most of the work for this part of the swing. Your club is back, your left shoulder is under your chin, your head is upright, your weight is shifted to right side, your wrists are hinged back with the club pointing down the target line, and your back is facing the target. Now you're ready to pull the trigger. Before you start the downswing, let's touch on one last item—relax.

My trigger method for starting the downswing is as follows: I start to throw my left hip toward the target while pulling down on the club in a very relaxed manner, allowing gravity and the acceleration of the tempo of my swing to do the work. The club and back end of the grip will be pointing at the golf ball. As I swing down, my hips shift laterally left and open to forty-five degrees or more through impact. The key is to keep my head behind the ball so that the coil of my shoulder and upper body, combined with the hinging of my wrists, can be timed for releasing the club at the proper time through the impact area. This will allow maximum power and accuracy. This is the part of the downswing that overlaps the last step of the golf swing, the follow-through.

As your club is released and approaches the impact area, the wrists should be starting to unhinge and the weight should continue to shift from the right to the left side to prepare for the swing finish (or follow-through, as I like to refer to it). Be careful not to release the hands and wrist too early or cast them at the ball because this will cause you to lose much of the power you stored in the backswing. The left side should remain firm just before and through the impact of the club head with the golf ball while the head remains behind the ball. When I am looking down at the ball as the club head is approaching impact, I look at the inside corner of the ball and try to keep a slight inside-to-out swing path by concentrating on hitting that inside part of the ball and aiming at one o'clock. I find that this will allow the club to drop into the power slot more readily and ultimately result in more distance and accuracy.

(**FORE Advice:** The information noted above is based on the assumption that the golfer is right-handed. Please reverse for left-handed golfers and note that the right hip will be moving toward the target.)

(**FORE Advice:** Keeping your left arm straight and your swing relaxed while keeping your head down and behind the golf ball through well after the contact point are key parts to more consistency in the golf swing.)

Step 7: The Follow-through

We have previously covered six of the seven steps in the seven-step swing checklist—the grip, the setup, the waggle, the backswing, tempo, and the downswing. And now the last step, but not the least in importance, is the follow-through or finish. All the steps are important, but if the follow- through is not done correctly it can negate the proper result of the other steps of the swing. As you approach impact with the golf ball during the downswing, make sure the acceleration of the club remains constant. This will be accomplished by acquiring a good tempo with your golf swing. Also on the downswing, as discussed in the last section, continue the path of the club through the ball on a slight inside-to-out path and aim at the one o'clock spot, as suggested. As you continue through the hitting zone after impact, keep the club as low as possible on this line. Your head should remain behind the ball. The hips should continue opening to the target, about sixty to seventy-five degrees or more at this point, and the weight of the lower half of your body should continue to shift onto your left side.

Pronate the hands and forearms - Club and arms should point down target line

If the follow-through is executed correctly, the club and your arms will form a line pointing at or slightly right or left of the target line. Both will be near parallel to the ground as your right shoulder starts to pass under your chin. The hands should pronate or turn over to the left just after the club passes through the impact zone. If you turn the hands over too quickly you may hook or draw the ball too far left and not achieve the result you were looking for. This is the part of the swing that takes practice and experience to master. Once you get the timing down, you will almost always be successful if you execute the rest of the steps correctly.

(**FORE Advice:** If you are consistently slicing the ball to the right side, you may want to consciously accentuate the turning of your hands over to the left as you reach impact, which should help correct this problem.) Another cause of slicing the ball to the right is not finishing the swing by staying on your right side and not letting the right foot come up onto the toe. See the information noted below regarding swing finish.

(**FORE Reference:** This is directed to the right-handed golfer and should be reversed for the left-handed player.) As your swing continues and your right shoulder is passing under your chin, the head can start to come up but the spine angle should remain intact as long as possible as you finish the swing. Your hips should now be almost fully open and perpendicular to and facing your intended target. (**FORE Advice:** Another key move at this part of the swing that is lacking in most beginners, and even some seasoned golfers, is moving to the left foot and finishing the golf swing. This means that the weight shift was never completed and the hips never rotated properly, causing a lack of both distance and accuracy.)

The proper execution of the follow-through includes the right foot pivoting up onto the toe, which means that the weight transfer from right to left is complete. The torso should be facing the target and the entire body should form some resemblance to a reverse C if you viewed it from a side perspective. The club should be wrapped around your neck and shoulders, and this pose should be maintained until the ball lands in the fairway or on the green. Holding this position will help promote the proper swing finish by making it part of your muscle memory, which will translate to a more accurate and repetitive finish to your golf swing.

**Reverse "C" Follow – Through – Pivot onto toe and face target.
Maintain this finish until the ball lands for more
consistent results.**

We have covered the seven-step checklist for the golf swing, and I hope it will be a help to your game. Some useful tips to remember and practice at the range and on the course are:

1. Tee the ball at the proper height (approximately half the diameter of the golf ball should be above the top of the driver as it lays at rest on the ground).

2. Keep your left arm straight.

3. Keep your head upright so that your chin does not interfere with the shoulder turn.

4. Make sure to finish your shoulder turn; if executed correctly, your back will face your target.

5. Make sure your wrist cocks back properly and your club is pointing back at the target.

6. Keep the head behind the ball for the majority of the swing sequence.

7. Pronate the hands just after impact. (FORE Advice: The pronation will happen naturally if you accelerate through the impact area and follow through correctly.

8. Make sure the right foot comes up on the toe at the finish and hold that position until the ball lands.

9. Relax your grip and release tension throughout your entire swing, and you will have a much better chance at success than with a tense body and stiff grip.

Take a deep breath and try to clear any unnecessary thoughts from your mind except the task at hand—striking the ball and landing it at the location you desire. Your golf swing will improve with practice and experience. Keep the faith!

CHAPTER 3

CURE YOUR SLICE

What is a slice? A slice is a shot that causes the ball to curve on a left- to-right path for the right-handed golfer, and the reverse is true for left- handed players. Depending on the severity of the slice, the ball may very well end up out of bounds, under the tree branches on either side of the fairway, or in some other hazard. This result would not be conducive to a good score on any golf hole. During my thirty-plus years playing golf, I have experienced the dreaded slice more times than you can imagine, both in my own game and the games of many beginning and seasoned golfers alike.

(**FORE Reference:** Any golfer can cause the ball to slice when they swing a golf club no matter how long they have been playing. It is a matter of using incorrect swing mechanics and is not dependent on the length of time or experience of the golfer.)

I have played with golfers who have been golfing for much longer than I have, but they still incorporate the slice in their swing. In fact, instead of attempting to correct the elements of their swing that promote the slice to begin with, they try to make adjustments in their setup, ball alignment, and grip to compensate for the slicing path of the golf ball. Some players have learned to play what I call a controlled slice, which is a slicing shot but played far enough to one side of the fairway or rough to allow the ball to land in play. The slice is a weaker shot that causes a loss of distance. I would not recommend this shot to any golfer whose goal is to acquire a low or scratch handicap. (**FORE Reference:** A handicap, as in bowling and some other sports, is the amount of stroke differential between players. See Chapter 13, Golf on a Bet: The Nassau—Not Just an Island in the Bahamas, for a more detailed explanation of handicap. A scratch golfer is a golfer who averages par, which is the number of strokes required to equal the score envisioned by the designer of the golf course.)

Having read many articles on this topic, viewed a variety of instructional videos, and tried out various swing techniques, I have discovered four key steps for correcting the dreaded slice.

Golf Swing Deficiencies that Cause the Slice

I would like to first discuss some of the swing deficiencies that can cause the slice. The slice can be caused by any or all of the following:

1. the grip—a weak grip
2. the setup—if the shoulders are open aligning to the target
3. the backswing—taking the club back on an improper path or swing plane
4. the follow-through—if the weight transfer from the right side to the left never occurs. If the hands do not pronate through the hitting area. If the right foot does not come up and pivot onto the toe. If the body is not facing the target at the end of the swing. (**FORE:Warning:** If any of the steps of the follow- through are not executed properly, it can further contribute to the severity of the slice.)

So I've kept you in suspense long enough. How do we rid ourselves of the slice? The four steps I have used successfully and recommend are:

1. Adjust your grip—A weak grip is one where the hands are turned too far to the left as the grip is taken. (**FORE**

Info: This would be for the right-handed golfer and the opposite would hold true for the left-handed player.) If the grip is taken properly, the first two or three knuckles of the left hand will be facing up and in view as you look down when addressing the ball. The meaty part of the right hand that is connected to the thumb will also be facing up and prominently in your view as you look down at your hands while completing the grip. (**FORE:** See Chapter 2, Step 1: The Grip, for more information.)

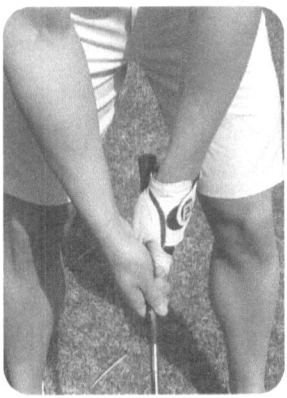

Strong Grip

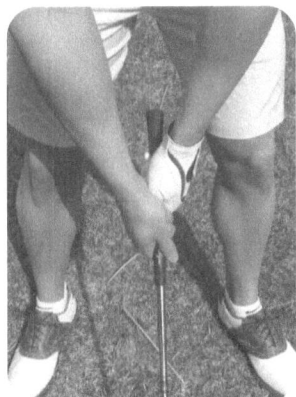

Neutral Grip

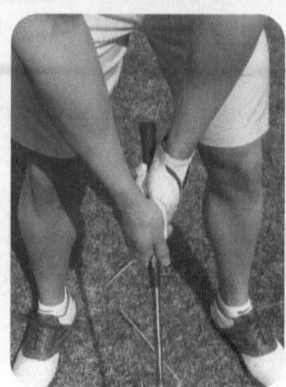

Weak Grip

2. Adjust your setup—The alignment of the shoulders and feet should be closed slightly, parallel to the target. Imagine a straight line drawn parallel to your feet and pointing down the target line. Pull your right foot back an inch or two, which will close your stance. This will cause the swing to have more of a tendency to produce a right-to-left ball flight.

3. The backswing—The backswing should be performed with more of an inside-to-out swing path, which will help move the ball from right to left instead of the opposite. (**FORE:** See Chapter 2, Step 4: The Backswing, for more information.)

4. The follow-through—(**FORE:** Make sure to perform all steps of the follow-through.)

a. The hands should pronate (turn over) through the hitting area.

Allow hands to (Pronate) turn over through the hitting area.

  b. The weight transfer from the right side to the left has to take place.

  c. The right foot must come up and pivot onto the toe.

Swing Finish or Follow- Through

  d. The body must be facing the target at the end of the swing and the finish held until the ball lands in the fairway.

These steps may feel uncomfortable at first, but if you practice them and make them part of your swing routine you will surely rid yourself of the slice. (**FORE Advice:** Do not give up.)

CHAPTER 4

SCHEDULING YOUR FIRST TEE TIME EVER

Proper Preparation

How do you know if you are really ready to play on a regulation golf course? If you think you are ready to schedule your first round on the golf course, let's take a moment to review what you have done in preparation to play. Have you purchased your golf equipment and, if so, do you have a checklist of all the items you will need to play? Golf clubs, bag, and golf balls are the most obvious, but a divot repair tool, ball markers, tees, a scorecard, and a pencil will also be required in order to play. Actually, the scorecard is only necessary as a reference for the distance from each tee location and golf rules for each hole, as it is not critical to keep an actual score your first few times out. You will receive a golf score card either at the pro shop where you check in and pay or from the starter who will give you one at the first tee while he advises you of the local rules of the golf course. If you have already acquired some proficiency at the game and you can keep your score within double par or better, then by all means mark your score.

Although not required by the rules of golf, a golf glove and golf shoes are two pieces of equipment that I highly recommend. They will add to your stability in gripping and swinging the golf club.

Have you taken golf lessons or taught yourself and practiced sufficiently to be able to achieve enough distance and accuracy to keep up with the pace of play required by local rules and course etiquette? Have you learned about the basic rules of golf and associated golf etiquette? Have you asked someone to join you who had played previously and is somewhat knowledgeable about how to play, the rules of golf, and golf etiquette? If you have answered yes to the above listed items, then I would say that you are ready to play your first round of golf. One last item that I would like to address is proper golf attire. Most golf courses have a required dress code. I recommend that you call ahead and find out the requirements so that you don't arrive at the course and get turned away or get asked to purchase a collared shirt and proper shorts or pants. Cutoffs, jeans, T-shirts, tank tops, etc., are not considered proper attire for the golf course, especially by country club standards. Wearing the proper golf attire is also another rule of golf etiquette.

A few of my recommendations for scheduling your first tee time are:

1. As noted previously, ask someone to join you who is familiar with the game and who knows the basic rules of golf and golf etiquette.

2. If you know someone who belongs to a country club and you can take advantage of this option, then request them to schedule a time for you when the course is the least crowded. This will allow you to feel less pressure, and it will give you some additional time to play. If not, drop by your local municipal course and check with the starter or local golf professional to see when he would recommend that you play for the first time. (**FORE Advice:** During the week and on weekends there are certain times that the golf course can be very crowded, which are not good times to play for the first time. In the afternoon, around 2:00 pm

to 4:00 pm, the course play is usually less busy, and it is a much better time to schedule your round.)

3. The standard time for a golf round for the average foursome is about four and a half hours or fifteen minutes per hole. Do your best to keep up with that pace of play. When you first start playing you might have a tendency to lose more balls on wayward shots and thus require more time to look for them, especially if you are playing a course with narrow tree-lined fairways. Do not take more than three to five minutes looking for a lost ball, and if you lose two or three in a row and there is a group behind you, then just drop a ball with the rest of your group and keep the pace of play moving. This is the main reason for suggesting the tee time to be scheduled on off hours so that it will be a more enjoyable experience for you and your fellow golfers. You will also be adhering to an important rule of golf etiquette by extending this courtesy.

Arriving at the Golf Course

As noted previously, the assumption is being made that all of the proper preparation has been made in order to make your first golf round as enjoyable as possible for you and your fellow golfers. Some of the measures to prepare for golf are worth repeating. For the sake of this writing we will assume you have purchased equipment (including proper golf attire), taken lessons, practiced sufficiently enough to play, and acquired some knowledge about the rules and etiquette of golf. That being said, I think you're ready to play.

If you have access to a private golf course or country club through a relative, friend, or colleague, then by all means take advantage of the accessibility to a golf setting that is not available to the majority of new golfers, especially for their first golf round. Ask them to set up a tee time for you and request them to play with you or have someone accompany you who is available and willing to play with a beginner and who knows the rules and etiquette of golf. If you do not have access to a private club and you are scheduling the tee time yourself, then I suggest you stop by the intended golf course and speak to the resident golf PGA professional and ask him for his recommendation on when to play. You can also speak to the golf starter who is in charge of sending out the golfers at the appropriate time and place on the course. He can advise you as to when to play so that you can enjoy the round without feeling pressured on every shot. Once you have scheduled your tee time, the next step is the arrival at the golf course. You should figure to arrive at the course at least a half hour before your scheduled time in order to allow for check-in and a warm-up, and especially if you would like to grab something to drink or eat before you play. As you enter the driveway to the course, you will most likely see directional arrows to the bag drop. Follow the signs so that you can unload your bag at the location nearest the course bag drop so that you will not have to carry your bag once you park the car. After you drop your bag, make sure to put your golf shoes on (if you have golf shoes, which is recommended) and proceed to the clubhouse and pro shop to register to play. You will then pay what are called "green fees" for either nine or eighteen holes (your preference) and proceed to the starter with your receipt so that he can set you up to play. Sometimes when the golf course is very crowded, the starter may elect to start some groups on the back nine, so be prepared for that possibility. This will occur at times, especially if you are only playing nine holes. It is actually a good idea for a new golfer to play nine holes for his or her first few times out. You can then request to be started on the tenth hole, thereby allowing you this part of the course to yourself. When I first taught my significant other to play, the starters were most cooperative and sent us off regularly on the back nine so that we would feel less pressured and not hold up the more advanced groups of players. The game of golf is meant to be played with a certain tempo and within a reasonable amount of time. If you are waiting on every hole, then you might lose your rhythm and not play as well as you may be capable of. This is an important part of golf etiquette that you will learn as you become more experienced with the game. Well, you've arrived at the golf course, dropped your golf bag at the bag drop, checked in with the pro shop and starter, and warmed up sufficiently. Are you now ready for the first tee?

Preparing for the First Tee

You have scheduled your tee time, arrived at the golf course, checked in with the pro shop and starter, and headed to the first tee. Congratulations! You are ready for the game of a lifetime. Once you are at the first tee there are some rules of etiquette that should be addressed here. There are varied placements of teeing areas, usually between two and five locations, so check the scorecard for distances of the different tee areas and total yardages that are set up for players of different skill levels and abilities.

The back tees are meant for the advanced player, usually with an established handicap of between 1 and 7, and the total yardage is usually between approximately 6500 and 7400 yards. The next forward tee box is normally for the experienced player who is between a 7 and 14 handicap, and the total yardage is normally between 6200 and 6700 yards. The next tee location is for the average golfer and can range from 5800 to 6300 yards, and the markers are normally white. Some courses have tee boxes for senior players and are usually gold or green.

Last is the women's tee location, whose markers are normally red in color and are usually the shortest on the course. This is not meant to be derogatory to the female golfers, because many of them can play from the men's tees and can hit a golf ball as well as and more accurately than many of their male counterparts. If a senior or female player is an experienced golfer, she can choose any tee area that is appropriate for her skill level. For new players or beginners, I strongly recommend the white or senior tees for the men and the red tees for the women. They allow you to play from a tee location that is reasonable for the beginning golfer. If you find you are scoring well right off the bat, then by all means move back to the next tee box for the next round. By scoring well, I mean close to par or better, and I personally don't think many beginners will fall into this category. In fact, I suggest that you do not keep score for the first few rounds. Give yourself some time to ease into the game. It will allow for a much more enjoyable experience and beginning of your journey into the wonderful world of golf.

Once you have selected your tee location, you must defer to the other players in your group and check if they are playing from the same location. If they are playing the tee locations farther back, they will hit first, and if they are playing the shorter tee locations, they will hit after you. When a player is on the tee box preparing to hit, the other players should stand off to the side and out of view of the golfer and remain quiet until he has completed his swing. This is one of the rules of golf etiquette and an important one to observe and remember. You will better understand my emphasis on etiquette as you become more experienced with golf. Also, the ball should be placed between the tee markers, either even with them or behind them, away from the golf hole, which is one of the rules of golf. It is not so important initially but it is good practice to abide by this rule as you learn to play. If you ever get into competitive golf, be sure to acquire knowledge of the basic rules or you might lose a match or tournament because your opponent calls you on an infraction of a rule you may not have been aware of. I wouldn't worry about it right now, though. Just play and enjoy the game.

Tee Time

It's tee time. Your first time teeing up and preparing to play can be a bit unnerving if you let it. It is human nature to be a little nervous when you are trying something new for the first time and people are around watching you. I have to admit when I first started playing I felt the same way. After a while you might realize that many players are also beginners and not much more experienced than you, so they are also nervous when it is their turn to hit in front of their fellow golfers. After a short time you will overcome your fear of the first tee. If you are having trouble at the first tee, you have some options. When my significant other started playing golf, she was petrified to hit in front of anyone. I explained my dilemma to the starter on the course and he was able to schedule us on the back nine or tenth tee where there were fewer players, if any, around. This was very helpful in easing her into the game, and it allowed her—and me for that matter—to enjoy a more leisurely round and initial golf experience. Soon she was an old pro, and the first tee jitters were gone. Another tip is to schedule your tee time when the course is less crowded, normally late morning or late afternoon, depending on the golf course. If you choose this option, it is a good idea to speak with your local golf professional or starter about when the optimal time for you to play is.

If no other options are available and you find yourself on the first tee, try to remember a few things. Everyone has to start somewhere, and I can guarantee that most beginners were no better than you when they started. Also remember the steps of your swing setup routine, and make sure you execute them all on each tee box. If you miss the ball, try once more and then pick up and drop your ball in the approximate area in the fairway near the other players in your group, an unwritten rule of golf etiquette. Another tip when on the tee is to relax. I don't mean to fall asleep over the ball, but just take a deep breath and exhale slowly before you swing the club. Try to clear your mind of everything but the task at hand, hitting the golf ball and your swing. If you have taken lessons and practiced sufficiently, you will feel more confident on the tee and have a better chance for a successful swing result. No matter how you do the first few times out, you should not be discouraged. If you really want to play golf, then you have to give yourself some time to acquire a knack for it and have patience at the beginning. If you have played other sports previously, then the game of golf usually—and let me emphasize usually—comes much easier than for those who have not played any sport before.

After teeing up your ball, pick an object a short distance in front of you that will align your ball with the intended target line of your landing area. Then set up your shoulders and chest parallel to that object and target line. This will increase your odds for a successful and accurate swing result, more so than just swinging the club at the ball without a target or goal in mind. Remember you are just beginning and, as much as I love the game of golf, it is not an easy game to master for most. It is a game, however, that can be played and enjoyed by players of any skill level. Give golf a chance, for it is truly the game of a lifetime.

CHAPTER 5

PLAYING YOUR FIRST GOLF ROUND EVER

The First Fairway

In the previous chapter we touched on the first tee jitters and some course courtesies of golf etiquette. The tee shot usually requires the use of the driver, which is the club with the least amount of loft and one that will allow you to attain the most distance. When using the driver, make sure all the steps in the seven-step checklist are followed to the best of your ability to allow the best chance for a successful drive off the tee. It is important to get the ball in play, as it will set a good tempo for the hole if you place the tee shot well and into or near the fairway. After you have hit your ball on the first tee along with your fellow golfers, the real game begins. I will continue to elaborate on some of the golf rules and etiquette of the game as we continue down the first fairway, so please pardon my redundancy. (**FORE Info:** Etiquette is defined as the courtesies extended to your fellow golfers both in your group and on the golf course, and to the golf course itself.)

One courtesy to be adhered to on the first tee, or any tee for that matter, is to remain quiet and stand to the side while another player is preparing to hit his shot. When all of the players in your group have hit their tee shots, you will go to the player's ball that is farthest from the green on that particular hole and allow him to hit first. The other players in the group or foursome—which is a common name for a group of golfers because the players are normally set up in groups of four— will stand off to the side, out of the view of the player who is about to hit or address the ball. This will allow them to maintain maximum concentration. It is very distracting when someone is beside the tee box talking or moving around, so remain still and quiet, an important rule of golf course etiquette. You will all then proceed to hit your second shots in order of who is farthest from the green—or "away," as referred to in golf lingo—while observing golf etiquette and no longer using a tee. The tee is the wooden or plastic device used to raise the ball to a desired height off the ground and can only be used for the first shot on each golf hole. The subsequent shots must be played where they lay in adhering to the normal rules of golf. In inclement weather conditions, after rain, or where there is standing water in the fairway or rough, the ball may be lifted, cleaned, and placed without penalty so that a player is not unfairly penalized for abnormal conditions on the course on a particular day. There are also winter rules and ground- under-repair situations whereby you may remove and replace your ball in a new location, no closer to the hole, without penalty. When you become proficient enough to play competitively, or even join a golf club, you must adhere to established rules and have everyone agree to the rules before you begin to play, or you may be called and penalized strokes or loss of a match because of an infraction of said rules.

When you approach your ball and prepare to hit your second shot, make sure you remember to align yourself with the target ahead. When the swing is executed properly many of the better players will take a divot, which is a section of grass or turf, and shoot it into the air as they complete their swing. Golf course etiquette dictates that the divot should be replaced or a mixture of seed and fertilizer be poured into the spot where the divot was taken. (**FORE Info:** Many players, especially beginners, will try to lift the ball into the air with their club instead of hitting the ball with a descending blow, which actually will cause the ball to rise up more proficiently, thus causing the divot to be taken.)

The correct swing for each person will come with practice under the guidance of a golf professional, whenever possible. A golf professional can help an individual attain a much more proficient swing in a much shorter amount of time than when self-taught. You can learn yourself, as I did, but the reading and the experimentation process usually takes much longer than being taught by a golf professional. After the second shot, you will proceed to hit the ball until you reach the green. The green is the tightly mowed area of grass around the flag stick or pin (another name for the flag stick, whichever terminology you prefer). The ball will then be putted into the hole in the least number of strokes possible, which will be discussed in the chapters to follow.

Options around the Green

Earlier in the chapter, we discussed scheduling your tee time, the first tee, hitting the ball in the fairway, some rules of etiquette, and approaching the green. The green, as noted previously, is the tightly mowed area of grass that surrounds the flagstick and cup. It is a most important area of the golf course because over half of your golf score will be determined by how well you do with your chipping, putting, and bunker or sand play on or around the green.

You now have hit your approach shot and you are on or near the green. The strategies utilized here will greatly affect how well you will score. If you are near the green and have a clear opening to the flag, then you have a few options in your approach. You can either use a more lofted club, such as a pitching, lob, or sand wedge, or you can utilize what is called the bump-and-run technique with a less lofted club, such as the 5-, 6-, 7-, 8-, or 9-iron. Tiger Woods sometimes uses a 4-iron, utilizing his putting setup and grip, and makes a smooth putting stroke in many cases around the green. It works well for him, as you can imagine. The more lofted clubs are harder for the new golfer to hit and achieve consistent results with accuracy and proximity to the cup. The professional golfer will use these clubs proficiently because of the hours of practice they have put in to perfect the feel with each club. When you have reached a certain level of expertise, you will know which club will work the best for you under any given shot requirement. In my opinion the bump and run, especially for the beginning golfer, will give you the best odds for getting closer to the cup if you are on the fringe or have a clear approach to the flagstick. The key to a consistently successful shot here is practice, as is the key with most any part of the game. The method I recommend for the beginner is to set up your body and alignment as if you were going to putt, maybe a bit open to the hole, which means your right shoulder and foot will be slightly forward of alignment to your left. (**FORE Advice:** This direction and those to follow are for right-handed golfers, and the opposite is true for left-handed golfers.)

Next, lean your weight toward your left side and set the ball slightly right of center toward your right foot. Close the clubface a bit and hit the ball as if you were hitting a putt but with a slightly more descending blow. This will be considered the bump. Make sure to follow through about the same distance as you took the club back to allow for the run, whereby the balls lands and rolls on the green, thus the term "bump and run."

Whether you use a 5-, 6-, 7-, 8-, or 9-iron will depend on distance and elevation of the green to the flag. If the green is sloping uphill, you will want to use a less lofted club, such as the 5-, 6-, or 7-iron to ensure additional roll after the ball lands to get up the inclined slope of the green. This will allow the ball to end up closer to the flag as the ball comes to a stop. If you have less green to work with or the green is sloping downhill, you will want to use a more lofted club, such as the 8- or 9-iron or pitching or lob wedge so that the ball will stop faster after it lands on the green. As stated earlier, the proper club selection for the varying distances will come with practice and playing time. One other tip that works well for me is to keep your head down until well after the ball is struck, and allow minimal body movement, as it is not required for this type of shot. The hips may rotate slightly open toward the target but minimally. Practice, practice, practice, and your consistency with this shot will develop with your experience as you play.

The Wedge Shot

In Chapters 1 through 5 we discussed all aspects of a player's first golf round, starting with the reservation of the tee time to the arrival at the course and the first tee box jitters. You now have advanced the ball to the greenside area. As noted in Chapter 5, Section titled Options around the Green, you can chip the ball with your irons or wedges and get close if you have some green and an opening to the flag location to work with. If you are in front of a sand trap or have some other obstacle between you and your target, it may call for another type of shot.

In order to overcome an obstacle in the way of your approach, such as a sand trap or tree, a different strategy is required. This shot will also depend on the amount of distance to the obstacle and the trajectory required to clear it and still reach the flag location. The most important thing to concentrate on is the shot at hand and the follow-through to a finished position. The strategy I use to get over an obstacle quickly is to set up with a higher lofted club, such as the sand or lob wedge, with the club nearer my left foot. I will then lay the clubface open so that the ball pops up faster than normal. The term "lay open" means the clubface is approaching a flat position with the blade pointing upward and a bit right in relation to your stance and the ground.

Lay Clubface Open

I also break my wrists back sharply and quickly, which also promotes height and less distance, your goal for this type of shot. Remember to follow through to a finished position or there is a good chance you will leave the shot short of your intended landing area. You can try this shot even if there is no obstacle in your way and get a feel for the line of ball flight you will achieve for future reference under actual playing conditions. How close you get to your target will be determined by the following: the distance away, your setup and grip techniques, and the amount of follow-through combined with the speed of your swing through the ball at impact. Accuracy and distance will come with practice, but the main goal is to get over the obstacle and onto the green and not land in a sand trap, a tree, water, or other hazard that may lay in front of you. This is one of the tougher shots required in golf, so if you master this one it will help your game and score tremendously. Practice is the key!

The Putt

The putt is the stroke or shot in golf used once your ball has landed on the green. This shot calls for rolling the ball toward the flagstick—or cup if the flag has already been removed—and is normally made using the putter. (**FORE Info:** The putter can be used from off the green while the flagstick is still in the cup.) The putter is the club that has the least loft and a relatively flat face. If you have been following all sections in Chapter 4 and 5, "Scheduling Your First Tee Time Ever" and "Playing Your First Golf Round Ever," respectively, then you have progressed from making your first tee time reservation, arriving at the golf course, overcoming the first tee jitters, hitting your clubs, progressing down the fairway, and finally reaching the green. Congratulations! You are on the green.

There are two key ingredients to making a good putt: speed and direction. Because the green usually slopes in different directions, a key element of putting is to learn how to read the slope of the green. The five main different types of putts normally encountered are: uphill, downhill, left to right, right to left, and straight. For an uphill putt, the ball must be struck harder in order to make it up the incline slope. The opposite holds true for a downhill putt because the ball will have a tendency to accelerate down the slope depending on the severity of the decline of that slope. A left-to-right putt will do exactly what it says, go from left to right. This means that you will aim your ball toward a target or line left of the cup, allowing the slope of the green to move the ball back toward the cup. The opposite holds true for a right-to-left putt. The amount of distance left or right again depends on the severity of the slope of the green. There are also double-breaking putts and even triple, which are usually associated with longer putts on very undulating greens.

When first starting to putt, I advise aiming directly at the cup or flagstick and experimenting to get a feel for both speed and direction. These two ingredients of putting are critical to ultimately scoring well at golf. More than half of the total strokes of a person's score are usually made on the putting green.

I strongly recommend that the beginning golfer spend some time on the practice green before teeing off. Check out the golf videos on putting available if you want to accelerate your learning curve. It is not as easy as it looks to groove a really good putting stroke without some effort and practice, which is key to all aspects of the game!

PART 2:

ADVANCING YOUR GAME–
THE BASICS OF GOLF PLUS

CHAPTER 6

CLUB RULES AND RANGE TIPS

Selecting Your Golf Clubs

There are fourteen clubs allowed by the USGA and PGA Rules of Golf that can be used during a round of golf. If you have more than the designated number you can be disqualified in tournament play. During a friendly golf round with your friends, and especially if you are trying out a new club, feel free to carry more than fourteen if so desired. Each club is a different length, and the clubface angle increases in proportion to the number of the club. The varied degree of the clubface is also known as the loft of the club. The different lofted clubs are used to attain the varied distances you will encounter to your target area in the fairway or to the green during your golf round. The driver has the largest head and the least amount of loft, usually 6 to 10.5 degrees, and is used to drive the ball for maximum distance, especially on the longer par 4, 5, and sometimes even par 6 holes.

The 3-, 4-, 5-, and 7-woods, the hybrids, and the irons have increasing degrees of loft and are angled respectively with the number of the club. Please note that as the number increases, the resulting distance will decrease proportionately. For example, a 9-iron will produce less distance than an 8-iron, and the 8-iron will be less than the 7-iron, and so on. The driver, or number 1 club, has historically been the most difficult club to hit with. With the new advancements and improved technology available today, the driver has become a much more reliable choice to use on most tee shots than a few years back.

I'm assuming if you're reading this guide, then you are just beginning to play golf and probably haven't hit too many golf balls. I would suggest that you visit the range once a week, if possible, and use the different clubs to try to gauge the average distance you can attain with each one. You can also keep a record of the distances reached so that you can use it as a reference when playing on the actual golf course. See the chart in Chapter 7 for a reference of the average distances noted for each club.

The Golf Range

The golf range is an excellent area to work on your golf swing and keep the golf muscles limber even if you don't have an opportunity to play on a golf course. (**FORE Advice:** Utilize your time at the range and don't just pull out the driver and start pounding balls as far as you can.) I always start with some warm-up exercises to keep from pulling any muscles, an important lesson I learned when I tore my hamstring while playing softball some thirty years ago. Although golf may not be as strenuous as other sports, such as football, hockey, and baseball, the back, arm, leg, and stomach muscles are used more than you may realize while swinging the golf club. It is good practice to warm up for five to ten minutes before you play to prevent injury. After the warm-up, I normally commence the practice session with my lob and pitching wedge because these are the easier clubs to hit. They will also allow you to get your tempo and rhythm going before using the longer-distance clubs that are harder to hit. (**FORE Advice:** Allow for a more productive range session by making sure you aim at a target and not just swing the golf club.)

There are various targets set up at most ranges, including greens and even flagsticks on some. Perform your setup routine from the seven-step checklist before each swing as a rehearsal for your next round on the golf course. It will be a much more productive experience if you are aligning your body and aiming at a specific target than if you are just swinging the club for the sake of swinging. Also, don't feel like you have to hit every club in your bag. For your first few trips to the range, select four or five clubs to use and purchase about eighty to a hundred balls to hit. Use approximately twenty to twenty-five balls for each club, and keep at it until you feel the results are consistent with each of them. **(FORE Advice:** As noted earlier, it is a good idea to gauge the distance you are attaining with the different number clubs. It will allow you to better select the proper club for the distance required when playing on the actual golf course.)

Whether you are using a pitching wedge, 9-iron, 7-iron, 5-iron, driver, 3-wood, 5-wood, hybrid, etc., try to have a game plan and goal of what you want to accomplish for your time spent at the range. I practice with each club until I feel I am getting the desired results for at least a half dozen shots or more in a row before I change to another club. Whenever possible, try to locate a range that has real grass hitting areas instead of mats because it more closely simulates actual course conditions and lies. **(FORE Advice:** Perform your setup routine before each shot on the range to stimulate muscle memory to prepare for actual course play.)

CHAPTER 7

GOLF CLUB DISTANCE GUIDE

Most new golfers are curious as to how far they are able to hit the golf ball with each club and how they might compare to other golfers. Because age, ability, athleticism, skill level, etc., are factors in the distance attainable for each player, the best way you can make this determination is to go to the range or have your instructor hook you up to a simulator and check the distance readings with various clubs. Since the range is more accessible, I would suggest this option for most new golfers.

I have included a chart for men and women depicting the *average* distances that I feel should be attainable for each club. (**FORE Info:** This information is purely an *average projection* derived from my thirty-plus years of experience playing with different golfers of all skill levels, ages, etc.)

CLUB	MEN'S CHART	WOMEN'S CHART
Driver	200 to 270 yards	150 to 210 yards
3-Wood	180 to 240 yards	140 to 190 yards
5-Wood	160 to 215 yards	130 to 170 yards
Hybrid	150 to 200 yards	120 to 160 yards

(**FORE Info:** Hybrids come in different lofts, so the distance noted on the chart is for a hybrid with similar characteristics to that of a standard 7-wood.)

4-Iron	160 to 190 yards	130 to160 yards
5-Iron	150 to 180 yards	120 to150 yards
6-Iron	140 to 170 yards	110 to 140 yards
7-Iron	130 to 160 yards	100 to130 yards
8-Iron	120 to 150 yards	90 to 120 yards
9-Iron	110 to 140 yards	80 to 110 yards
Pitching Wedge	90 to 130 yards	70 to 100 yards
Sand Wedge	80 to 110 yards	60 to 90 yards
Lob Wedge	50 to 90 yards	40 to 70 yards

(**FORE Info:** The lob wedge also comes in varying degrees of loft, approximately fifty-four to sixty degrees.) I have also deliberately not included distances for 1-, 2-, or 3-irons because I feel they are more difficult to hit and should not be used by the beginning or average golfer, especially since the introduction of the hybrid clubs.

A putter can be used to advance the golf ball toward the flagstick or cup even when the ball rests off the green. This is not on the chart since the distance the putter will advance the ball will come from practice and experience. (**FORE Advice:** I do not recommend using the putter in high grass or if any hazard lies between your ball and the flagstick.)

The distances noted on the charts listed above are for average golfers, especially beginners. It does not take into consideration wind conditions, humidity in the air, etc., which can definitely be a factor in how far the golf ball will travel. Please do not be disillusioned if you cannot hit as far as any of the distances listed here. It is just a projection of my experience with the average and new golfer over the past thirty years and can vary depending on age, strength, athleticism, swing speed, technique, and a number of other factors.

For instance, professional golfers, both women and men, can drive the ball well over 250 to 300 yards or hit a 7- or 8-iron 170 to 200 yards or more if they so desire. So do not judge your distance by the statistics of the golf professional. They will not be proportionate nor are they required to play golf.

The average golfer does not need to achieve these distances to have a good game and enjoy the sport. The distance will come with experience and practice, which will also promote accuracy. This is most important for a good and consistent golf game. Distance is negated if the ball is hit off line into the woods or out of bounds. Don't worry so much about distance; work on swing technique to achieve greater accuracy, and the length will naturally follow.

CHAPTER 8

WIND SHOTS AND
UNEVEN LIES

The previous chapter noted some average distance projections with each club, but what do you do when the wind is blowing against you? Depending on the severity of the wind you may opt to select a club one, two, or even three times stronger than normal to neutralize the effects of the wind blowing in your direction. For example, if you normally hit a 7-iron 150 yards and the wind has kicked up and is blowing in your direction, you may want to select a 6-, a 5-, or even a 4-iron instead and swing at your normal swing speed and tempo. You'll still reach your 150-yard goal in distance.

(**FORE Advice:** Do not try to force the shot or you will end up lifting the ball higher in the air and losing even greater distance than with your normal swing.) Instead, you can set the ball a bit farther back in your stance, choke down a little farther than normal, and select the less-lofted clubs to help neutralize the effects of the wind. It also helps to choose an even stronger club and swing to a three-quarter finish. This should provide a lower trajectory, which will result in a more penetrating shot into the wind. The opposite holds true if the wind is behind you and blowing toward your intended target. In this case you would select one or two clubs less and allow the wind to carry the ball the balance of the distance. As noted before, if you normally hit your 7-iron 150 yards and the wind is behind you this time, then drop to an 8- or even a 9-iron if the wind is strong enough.

(**FORE Advice:** Here's a good thought when golfing in the wind: Make your normal swing, but change the club selection higher or lower and adjust your alignment right or left to offset the intensity of the wind in either direction.) While on the topic of wind, you will also encounter a right-to-left and a left-to-right wind at various times when you play. Although this type of wind can also affect distance, your alignment adjustment would be more important in this case. If the wind is blowing from right to left, align your body slightly right of the intended target line to offset the effect of the wind; the opposite would hold true if the wind was blowing left to right. Align your setup more left in this case. If the wind is really intense, you might want to choose one club stronger than normal to offset the potential loss of distance the wind may cause.

Uneven Lies

Besides wind, another shot that you will encounter in golf is the uneven lie. It can be a side hill, downhill, or uphill shot; all require adjustments with your setup to compensate for the effects of the uneven lie. They may also require a change in club selection because you could lose or gain distance depending on various factors. For instance, if the ball is on a downhill lie, then the resulting loft of the golf club is proportionately decreased with the severity of the slope of the hill. In order to overcome this condition you need to make certain adjustments in club selection to compensate for the slope. If you are away from the hole that same 150 yards and your normal club would be a 7-iron, drop to an 8-iron or even a 9-iron, again depending on the severity of the down slope and you should still be able to reach your target.

(**FORE Advice:** Using a higher lofted club will also aid in getting the ball in the air, as the downhill lie can cause the ball to be easily topped if the swing of the club is not along the line of the slope.) It will also be beneficial to take a three-quarter swing to ensure stability on the uneven terrain. Adjusting club selection will also allow the ball to get into the air more readily and increase the possibility of a more accurate line, even if slightly short of the target. This is another condition you will encounter on the golf course. Overcoming these obstacles will come with practice and experience, which will determine what works best for you. The opposite strategy would be true for an uphill lie. Select a club or two stronger than normal. For example, instead of using the 7-iron for that 150-yard shot, use a 6- or even a 5-iron, again depending on the severity of the upward slope toward the target. The upward slope will add additional loft to the club, thus resulting in less distance than normal. I also recommend swinging to a three-quarter finish, as the full-swing finish has a tendency to lift the ball higher in the air and negate distance, which you do not want in this particular situation.

You will also encounter side hill lies, both upward and downhill as course layout will dictate. For the down-sloping side-hill lie, your swing and contact will have a tendency to push the ball right, so line up left of your intended target line and move the position of the ball more to center in your stance to offset this tendency.

The opposite would be true for an uphill side-hill lie. The ball will have a tendency to go left of your target when you use your normal setup, so aim right of your target line and also more to the center of your stance to compensate. The amount of distance, either left or right, again depends on the severity of the slopes, whether up or down.

(FORE Advice:

- Uphill side-hill lie—Choke up on the club, and use one or two clubs stronger to help maintain alignment. The slope will cause the side-hill lie to push the club shaft up, closer to you and above your feet.
- Downhill side-hill lie—Use a club or two stronger, which will also be longer in length, and grip the club toward the upper part of the grip to keep the spine angle more upright

and lessen the reach factor required to play the ball on the downhill slope.

- No matter what uneven lie you may encounter—uphill, downhill, side hill/up slope, or side hill/down slope— remember to *swing along the slope of the ground* in each case to the best of your ability.)

The driving range cannot simulate this type of shot. If the golf courses near you are hilly or mountain layouts, and if you are self-taught, I recommend that you try to find an open area in your neighborhood where there are some hills and practice hitting balls off the different lies, as noted above. Monitor the various adjustments in your setup, stance, club selection, etc., required for you to successfully execute the shots under the different conditions encountered. If you opt for lessons with a PGA professional, you can explain to him the conditions on your local golf course so that he can advise you as to how to better overcome them. There are instructional manuals and golf videos, which will also show you how to adjust your stance, setup, club selection, etc., for these conditions. (**FORE Advice:** *Golf Digest* offers many strategies and tips on the various conditions noted above, including wind shots and uneven lies. Visit www.golfdigest.com for valuable tips and golf info.)

When first learning to play golf, it is prudent to play on a reasonably flat golf course whenever possible until you get some experience behind you. On the other hand, playing on a hilly course may help you become a better player sooner. It will allow you to experience various shot requirements and thus be better prepared to overcome them on any of the courses you will encounter in the future while playing golf. I listed these types of golf shots because they are some of the tougher ones I encountered when I first learned to play. They are still tough shots, but with the alignment and club selection changes that you can make, it will provide you with a much better chance for a successful outcome, which is the goal of this golf guide. (**FORE:** Relax, practice, and most of all enjoy golf!)

CHAPTER 9

RELAX—A KEY TO THE GOLF SWING

In Chapter 2, I wrote about the seven-step swing checklist. The one key ingredient to all of the seven steps is to relax. It is a natural tendency for most of us to try to muscle or power the ball toward the hole. I did it for many years with sporadic success. I was tired of hitting one good shot in five and not scoring the way I knew I was capable of. I am an avid reader of golf magazines and have more than once come across articles stressing the relaxing of the muscles, especially in the hands, forearms, shoulders, and chest, used during the golf swing in order to attain better results. I decided to go to the range and see if I could try this relaxed method of the golf swing. There was an immediate improvement. Once I incorporated relaxation into my golf swing, the percentage of successful strokes increased proportionately with the greater distance achieved. I was amazed at how much farther and more accurately the ball traveled with my newfound relaxed swing method. Let me pause here for a minute and explain my definition of relaxation. Relaxing during the golf game and golf swing does not mean to fall asleep while addressing the ball. It does mean, however, to clear your mind of distracting thoughts and tense muscles to whatever degree possible. It means to let the club drop into the power slot naturally and let the speed of your swing and relaxed muscles help you to achieve the desired result. I found that the club released and accelerated more on line when I maintained a light grip and little upper body stiffness or tension than if I tried to power the ball toward the target, which many times resulted in a missed shot to the left or right. The only thought that should be in your mind is the proper execution of the swing to produce the desired result for the golf shot at hand. Whether the stroke is a drive off the tee or a finesse shot over a bunker to a tight pin placement, focus on executing the shot and achieving the desired result.

I was always very competitive at sports and wanted to hit the ball the best and the farthest in baseball and golf, which is a natural inclination when you are used to competitive play. The tendency for many of us is to try to rip into the ball with all the power we can muster. In baseball you can get away with it more easily, but the speed and timing of a relaxed swing, even in baseball, will achieve better and more consistent results than tight muscles and a forced swing. This is most especially true for the golf swing. "Swing easy and hit hard!" That is my motto. There are different methods for relaxing before and during a golf round. During the round I have found that a deep slow breath—inhale and exhale—on about a seven- second count for each as I line up my shot from behind the target will help promote a relaxed swing for me. I then make one rehearsal swing utilizing that technique and then step up and hit before over-contemplating the swing. Too much time over the ball allows negative thoughts to creep into your mind and almost always results in a poor shot. The player who is confident in his or her abilities will address the ball, perform the setup routine, and proceed to swing without taking an inordinate amount of time over the ball. Practicing the various golf shots you will come across during any particular golf round will also help build confidence when that situation actually occurs during play.

Another method of relaxing I use is listening to music the night before or the morning of my golf round. Whatever type of music you like should work for you. I know it helps clear my mind of any unnecessary or stressful thoughts.

Happy golfing and relaxation to all!

CHAPTER 10

GOLF—THE COLLATERAL BENEFITS OF THE GAME

In previous chapters of this guide, I stated that I had been playing golf for about thirty years or so. For the first thirteen years of the thirty, I played the game but never realized the collateral benefits derived from playing golf. I used to arrive at the golf course, set up my bag and clubs on the golf cart, proceed to the course, and beat that little white ball around until it got into the intended hole. Golf was meant to be a fun and delightful experience, not one of frustration or anger because the ball did not respond to your every whim and command. For the new or beginning golfer who has not experienced the roller-coaster ride of emotions and frustrations that you can encounter during a round of golf, don't be disheartened; you soon will. That is unless you employ the proper mind-set right from the beginning and do not take the game too seriously.

I planned my first golf trip in April 1990 and decided to go to Myrtle Beach, South Carolina, the golf capital of the world. My experience on that trip gave me a whole new perspective of the game. I guess you can say it was a turning point in my perception of what golf was really all about. You can think of golf as just a game, like I did for the first thirteen years playing, or you can realize and enjoy the more obscure collateral benefits of playing golf. What are these benefits? you ask. Take the time to stop and smell the roses. What do I mean by that? Most golf courses are designed utilizing the natural beauty of the surrounding terrain as a backdrop. Besides the intrinsic beauty of the course itself, you can often see nature at its best. When I started visiting Myrtle Beach and subsequently Florida, the wildlife and surrounding fauna and plant life were incredible, not to mention the huge sprawling elms, oaks, and magnificent cypress trees and palms, whose mere existence and appearance exuded a climate of an exhilarating and at times exotic nature. Speaking of nature, there has been many a morning that I have ventured out onto the golf course only to encounter a family of deer meandering across the fairway or grazing in the adjacent brush to any particular golf hole. Some of my most memorable experiences, where I have encountered nature at its best, were at

- Pawley's Plantation (near Pawley's Island, in the south part of the Grand Strand, and a Jack Nicklaus design)
- The Witch (off of Route 544)
- Oyster Bay (located in North Myrtle Beach).

The first time I played The Witch with my significant other in the early 1990s, it was an eerie but exhilarating experience. I normally schedule our tee times early, around 7:00 am, so that we can play thirty-six holes if we so desire. When we arrived at the course, we signed in at the pro shop, checked in with the starter, and were sent out to the first tee. The first tee is a good distance from the clubhouse, which by the way is built in the shape of a witch's hat. A few minutes later we arrived at a secluded area at the first tee. It was prior to sunrise and I would guess about a quarter mile or so away from the clubhouse. There was a misty fog hovering over the landscape for as far as the eye could see. It appeared to be everywhere and it blanketed the cart paths and the entire golf course. This added an eerie, almost spooky Halloween-like feeling, but it was a very appropriate ambiance for The Witch. After all, the course was named The Witch. How much more appropriate can you get? Once the sun rose and the fog burned off, the course returned to its normal beauty and persona. On the next hole we were greeted by an alligator attempting to make some unsuspecting bird his prey. I guess the bird was flying too low over one of the ponds where the gator lived and he was looking for breakfast. Luckily for the bird, he got away. I have seen more than a few dozen alligators in my last nineteen years or so visiting Myrtle Beach and Florida. Most of the time, the gators were resting peacefully alongside the golf hole, sunning themselves. Even though an alligator may appear to be sleeping, I do not recommend retrieving a golf ball that may have come within close proximity to him, or near any wetlands for that matter. Although I only mentioned three courses as my most memorable experiences, almost every course we have visited has so much to offer in the way of natural beauty and wildlife, not to mention the intrinsic beauty of the golf courses themselves. Many golf courses provide homes to varied forms of wildlife, including families of turtles, ducks, geese and alligators, that abound in their ponds and many man-made and natural lakes and streams alike.

Swans, ospreys, egrets, eagles, falcons, hawks, and so many other species of birds too numerous to mention also abound in and around the courses in the temperate southern climate of Myrtle Beach and Florida. Since vacationing in Myrtle Beach almost twenty years ago, I have enjoyed the experience of golf so much more. The game of golf in itself is a wonderful experience, but coupled with the beauty of nature, the wildlife, and plant life that is so plentiful on most courses, it provides an unbeatable combination that complements the enjoyment of the game splendidly. While playing a game that I enjoy more than any other on the planet, the exhilaration of the experience is now magnified many times since I have learned to stop and smell the roses during the course of my round. We all want to play well, but the enjoyment of the golf experience should be your first priority and not just what you score on the card. Take a tip from me: The next time you are on a golf trip or visiting your local course, stop and smell the roses. It will add a different perspective to a game that you may have never realized or appreciated before.

I would like to mention perhaps another more important collateral benefit of the game. Golf can be a frustrating and delightful experience at the same time. One or two holes you might play well and then wonder what transpired on the next when you double bogey or worse. It's the nature of the game. When I am having a bad day on the golf course, I recall a book given to me that taught me some very important aspects of the game. Golf can be a game of self-enlightenment and about life. I feel compelled to recommend the aforementioned book that my sister and mother gave me as a birthday gift about a year or so ago. It is *Golf for Enlightenment: The Seven Lessons for the Game of Life* by Deepak Chopra. I had heard of Mr. Chopra before, but I am an avid fan of his now. If you take this somewhat spiritual journey with Adam and Leela, Mr. Chopra's characters in the book, you might be amazed to see how playing the game of golf could relate to the game of life itself. He can tell it so much better than I can. It is a book I highly recommend for both the beginner and experienced golfer. You can visit his Web site at www.chopra.com or www. randomlargeprint.com.

His book can help you immensely with your outlook on the game of golf, which in turn will provide you with a much greater chance for success in both the game of golf and maybe life itself. As always, happy golfing to all!

PART 3:

PLANNING A GOLF TRIP

CHAPTER 11

MY GOLF TRAVEL EXPERIENCES AND RECOMMENDATIONS

Myrtle Beach, South Carolina—Top-Rated Golf Destination, Vacation Spot, or Both?

In the winter of 1990, I was contemplating planning my first golf vacation. At that time I had been playing for about thirteen years, approximately once a week at Marine Dunes Golf Course in Brooklyn on Flatbush Avenue. Another course I played often was Dyker Beach Golf Course in Bensonhurst, Brooklyn, which at the time was the most played public course in the country.

I always wondered what it would be like to go on vacation for an entire week and be able to play golf every day if I wanted to. In conversation with my golf club comrades and by reading my favorite golf magazines, *Golf Digest* being at the top of the list, it became clear to me that Myrtle Beach would be a great choice. I had one dilemma, which was the fact that my significant other was joining me on the trip and had never played golf before. I offered her this option: Learn to play golf or wait for my return while I play for five or six hours.

She was athletic and into sports—softball, baseball, and football—as I was, so she opted to learn to play. Her decision to learn to play posed my second dilemma, which was how to teach her in four or five weeks before we had to embark on our trip. A crash course with an instructor? Or should I take on the challenge? I presented her with the choice, and the next thing I knew we were in the local ball fields after work and on weekends, and I was teaching her to play. She actually progressed better than I would have imagined. She was hitting an 8-iron about 125 to 130 yards, and pretty straight at that. Some of the guys I played with did not hit that well. She had one last query before we left on our trip, especially since she had never played golf. That was, "Are there other things that we can do besides golf?" Good question, but I had already anticipated it and I was ready. Of course there are other things to do: I heard the beaches were beautiful; miniature golf, which she enjoyed, was readily available; water parks were in abundance; there were great restaurants; and I saved my ace in the hole for last—there were plenty of places to shop.

That did the trick. We were ready, so Myrtle Beach, here we come! In April 1990 we were off to our first-ever golf vacation. We stayed at the Ocean Dunes Resort and had reserved an oceanfront room with a balcony overlooking the beach, which turned out to be a very good decision on our part. If you have a few extra dollars and enjoy the beach and ocean, it's well worth the additional cost. We are usually early risers and we thoroughly enjoyed the sunrise each morning as we anticipated our day. Then on to breakfast, a nice little buffet, which was included in our golf package. All it cost additionally was a few dollars for the tip. Finally, the golf was incredible. The first golf course we ever played at Myrtle Beach was Buck Creek, now renamed Aberdeen. Then we played Long Bay, a Jack Nicklaus design and highly recognizable in many golf magazines at the time, especially his signature tenth hole. Next was Tidewater, which we thoroughly enjoyed. It is one of my favorite golf courses played to date. We also played a few others, each one better than the next. Since this was her first time playing, Cathi was a little nervous on the first tee, as all the other players were milling around waiting for their turn to play. Realizing our situation, the starter, who on most courses is usually personable and considerate, set us up on the back nine where no one was around. This courtesy was greatly appreciated and made the experience much more enjoyable than it would have been otherwise. I strongly recommend to the new golfer to let the starter at the course know that you are just beginning to play. Let him know you would appreciate if he can place you where the least number of golfers are playing, if possible. Some golf course complexes have more than eighteen holes, such as Myrtle Beach National, Barefoot Landing Resort, Legends, Arrowhead, and Heather Glen, to name a few. One of their nine-hole layouts might be more readily open for you to play. This is not always the case, but you have the option to schedule your tee time when the course is less crowded. This would allow you a more relaxed atmosphere in which to play, as you could take a little more time if necessary. The dining was also very enjoyable, as we had some fine meals at Gullyfield's, which is no longer in existence. We also visited Rossi's, a nice Italian venue with music, including a little Dean and Frank and conveniently located at the Galleria Mall off Route 17. Rossi's also offered atmosphere and ambiance with an Italian flair as you enjoy your meal. Damon's, for the rib lovers, was another good choice and was located at Barefoot Landing at the time. Damon's has since relocated and is bigger and better than ever. Lastly, we dined at my favorite restaurant on the beach, Greg Norman's Australian Grille, also located at the Barefoot Landing Shopping Complex, about a mile or so north of where Route 22 and Route 17 (Kings Highway) meet. I'm not sure if Greg's Place was open at that time, but it has since been a must-stop for us over the last few years. The Australian Grille offers the option of dining inside or outside the restaurant, which overlooks the Intracoastal Waterway. The outside offers a bit more relaxed and less noisy atmosphere, complete with lighted trees, gas torches, an outdoor fireplace, entertainment, and a view of the sunset as you dine if you time it right. What more can you ask for? The shops at Barefoot Landing are varied and offer a multitude of choices for dining, clothing, fudge, taffies, and all kinds of souvenirs. Klig's Kites and the Christmas Mouse are two of our favorite shops to visit. We always find some great seasonal flags, Christmas souvenirs, and gifts to bring home.

Our first few trips to Myrtle Beach were so centered around golf that we never realized how enjoyable a day at the beach could be. Before golf, Myrtle Beach's reputation as a seaside resort was well known and attracted many visitors each year. Even for the most die-hard golfer, which I would pretty much consider myself, I highly recommend a day of relaxation and fun at the beach. Rent a lounge chair and umbrella, toss the football or Frisbee around, enjoy the beauty of the ocean and the waves, or just sit, relax, have a beer or two if you'd like, and take in all the sights around you. I promise you won't be disappointed. Since the sport of golf has become an integral part on the makeup of Myrtle Beach, it really has become a family vacation spot and golf destination that the entire family can enjoy.

There is golf, the beach, water parks, rides, miniature golf, restaurants, and shopping complexes, such as Barefoot Landing and Broadway at the Beach. Broadway at the Beach also has many shops, restaurants, mini- golf courses, rides, and entertainment, including the Hard Rock Cafe.

There are also nightspots for the younger and middle-aged crowd and a multitude of other enjoyable choices, including Ripley's Believe It Or Not! and the Aquarium, which is fun for all ages. When the sun is down, the die-hard golfers can also enjoy Medieval Times, the Carolina Opry, Alabama Theatre, and Dolly Parton's Dixie Stampede, which are just a few of the other options providing entertainment for the entire family, golfer, and non-golfer alike.

For the family vacation, many of the hotel golf packages and golf courses offer *free* golf for children and young adults aged sixteen and under when accompanied by a paying adult, which is not a bad deal.

Some of my favorite but more high-priced courses to play are Tidewater (as mentioned previously), Caledonia, and True Blue, two beautiful Mike Strantz design gems. Some other favorites are TPC, Kings North at the Myrtle Beach National Resort, and Pawley's Plantation, located at the southern end of the Grand Strand and designed by Jack Nicklaus, my favorite golfer of all time. With over 130 golf courses located within a 30- mile radius, it's no wonder that Myrtle Beach is known as the golf capital of the world. If you are planning a golf or family vacation, check out Myrtle Beach. I'm sure you will revisit it for many years to come. Happy golfing and vacationing to all!

My Top Ten Golf Courses in Myrtle Beach

1. Caledonia Golf and Fish Club—designed by Mike Strantz, formerly a member of Tom Fazio's Golf Design team, and an excellent designer in his own right. This South Strand golf course has it all.
2. Tidewater—a close second and another one of my all-time favorites anywhere. The closest you'll get to Pebble Beach on the Strand.
3. True Blue—Mike Strantz has two in my top ten and deservingly so. The sister course to Caledonia and another gem on the South Strand.
4. Heritage—Its beauty and layout will rival most. Worth the price of the ticket.
5. Grande Dunes—Located off 17 Bypass, this track is worth the time and money to try at least once.
6. The Dunes—one of the top-ranked courses in the world and a former stop on the Senior Tour. Also highly recommend to play at least once.
7. Pawley's Plantation—a Jack Nicklaus design and one of my favorites on the Strand. The layout is not for the faint of heart. You'll either love it or hate it; not usually any in-betweens on this one.
8. Myrtle Beach National King's North Course—an Arnold Palmer design. What more can I say? The other two courses in this fifty-four–hole complex, South Creek and the West Course, are not bad either and great for replays when King's North is booked.
9. World Tour—a twenty-seven–hole complex whose design is derived from some of the top-rated golf hole layouts in the world, including Augusta National and the Old Course at St. Andrews. This one caters to the golfer. A bit pricey,

but if you're not a world traveler or do not have access to Augusta National, you may want to check it out.

10. Barefoot Landing Golf Complex—Fazio or Dye courses. This one's a tie. Can't lose with either option. Includes four courses in all (seventy-two–hole complex). The Love Course is good and the Norman course is okay, but Fazio and Dye have them beat.

Disney World: Land of Make-Believe and Golf Too

We have to give credit to Mr. Walt Disney, whose ability to manifest his dreams is second to none. Walt—or out of respect, Mr. Disney—opened Disney Land in Anaheim, California, in the mid-fifties, at just about the time the Brooklyn Dodgers were leaving their fans in Brooklyn and heading for Los Angeles, California. His vision was not yet complete, for he had found a perfect piece of property in Orlando, Florida, where he would initiate the creation of the most magical land on the face of the earth. This was also the place where another and maybe final portion of his dream would be realized. In the spring of 1990, I had planned my first golf vacation ever to Myrtle Beach. It was such a wonderful trip that I was soon ready for another. While I was contemplating my next golf vacation destination, slated for the late summer or fall of 1990, my significant other came up with what later turned out to be an excellent suggestion. "How about Disney World?" I said, "I have never been to Disney World, or Disney Land for that matter, but what about golf?" I was reminded that the Buick Classic, which I think it was called at the time, was played at Disney World, so *duh*, there must be golf courses there, right? Yes, there were. In fact, Disney World was a stop on the PGA Tour since opening in the early seventies. The Magnolia and the Palm were the two courses that highlighted the tournament. There is also Lake Buena Vista, a course less known but one that turned out to be very enjoyable to play. I was convinced that we should give it a shot. What could we lose?

In September 1990 we were headed for what turned out to be one of the best vacations ever. We booked our hotel right on Disney premises at the Disney Inn, a quiet little section of the adjacent resort to the two main golf courses, the Magnolia and the Palm. A few years later, the inn was turned over to the U.S. government. It is my understanding that it is now utilized for the armed services entertainment and supplementary needs.

We were disappointed when we couldn't make our future reservations there because it was a sequestered resort where we could enjoy peace and quiet. We now frequent the other resorts, especially Port Orleans, French Quarter, which is centrally located and reasonably priced. Although not quite as sequestered as the Disney Inn, it provides a certain amount of privacy, beauty, and just the right touch of ambiance in the surroundings to be very enjoyable as well. In the process of booking our golf reservations, we were advised that there were two other newer courses at the Bonnet Creek Resort, not too far from where we were staying. They were named Eagle Pines and Osprey Ridge and were designed by two of the premier architects of the time, Tom Fazio and Pet Dye, respectively. Having kept up with my *Golf Digest* subscriptions, I was well versed in the reputation of these two golf architects. It dawned on me that I had just recently read about the openings and rave reviews received when they had first opened a short while ago. Since we were able to visit Disney World for six days, it allowed us enough time to play a different course every day and one course twice if we chose to. Luckily, we were able to reserve tee times at the two new courses at Bonnet Creek. So, our room, airfare, rental car, and tee times were booked as we waited impatiently for the next few months to go by so that we could venture off to another unforgettable golf vacation.

Unforgettable is just what it turned out to be. Our days there commenced with awakening in a magnificent suite at the Disney Inn Resort, which included a view of Snow White and the Seven Dwarfs carved into the hedges outside our room. It was also very enjoyable to view the sunrise each morning with a view of a water feature in the courtyard area outside that was landscaped with beautiful and exotic plant life and fauna. Then we were off to a cheery musical breakfast fare at the Contemporary Resort where Mickey, Minnie, Donald, Pluto, Goofy, and Chip 'n' Dale entertained and joined us for some fun. Last, but certainly not least, the anticipation of playing golf on any one of five magnificent golf venues, each one better than the next. How could you beat it? We enjoyed every one of the golf courses, especially the two new Bonnet Creek courses, Eagle Pines and Osprey Ridge.

After golf, we enjoyed a quick lunch at the Clubhouse Dining Room, which overlooked the golf course. But the fun had just begun. It was off to one of the magical parks that are part of the Disney World Resort.

We visited every park: Magic Kingdom, MGM, Animal Kingdom, and Epcot. Like the golf courses, we enjoyed each one more than the next. I was thirty-eight years old when I first visited Disney World, but age did not matter. Whether some of us want to admit it or not, we are all children at heart, and that is a good thing. It allows us to enjoy the rides, exhibits, entertainment, characters, parades, fireworks, and the rest without the inhibition of feeling foolish. The high points of my park experiences were the Carousel of Progress in Magic Kingdom, where I reminisced of my preteen years when I first viewed it at the World's Fair in Flushing Meadows, Queens, in 1963–1964. Then it was off to Fantasmic! and the Sci-Fi restaurant at MGM; the Laser Light Show and Pavilions of the World at Epcot; and the Tree of Life, A *Bug's Life* 3-D show, and "Tarzan" at Animal Kingdom. The "Tarzan" show was awesome and a must-see if you visit Animal Kingdom during your stay at Disney World. There are so many other wonderful things to see and do at the parks, too numerous to mention. If you are planning a family vacation or just a getaway for yourself or for you and your significant other, make Disney World a choice for your next trip. If golf is on your itinerary, I can attest from my own experience, you won't be disappointed. (**FORE Advice:** If you stay on the premises and book your tee times after a certain time, around 10:00 am, you may be able to receive discounted rates on green fees. There are also twilight rates in the afternoon that are priced at a reduced rate.)

While on vacation at Disney World, our daily agenda included playing golf, visiting the parks in the afternoon after golf, between 3:00 and 5:00 pm, and staying well into the evening to enjoy the nightly parades, light shows, and fireworks displays. Since this was my first visit there, I did not want to miss out on any of the magic that Disney World has to offer. I have tried to make Disney World an annual or biannual stop since my first visit, and I never tire of the excitement and magical experiences that the resort has to offer.

Bravo to Mr. Disney! He had a wonderful dream that we all can share and benefit from, thanks to his fortitude and ability to make that dream come true. Happy golfing and vacationing to all!

Las Vegas: Gambling, Golf, and Good Times

In previous sections, I spoke about Myrtle Beach and Disney World, which are two excellent choices for golf and vacation destinations—no two ways about it. I had been alternating between both places for about ten years and had some great times, but we were ready for a change, for something different. Where would we go next? I had always wanted to return to Las Vegas since my first visit there in 1976, but I just never had the opportunity. I had stopped in Las Vegas for three days on my return trip home from my honeymoon in Hawaii, my favorite place on the planet, met some friends there, and had a blast. In 2002, my fiftieth birthday was quickly approaching and my significant other surprised me with a gift that I did not expect, a four-day golf trip to Las Vegas. Could it get any better? I guess maybe a five- or six-day trip would have been better, but she wanted to make sure we did not go broke while we were there, so four days was a good compromise. We were staying at the MGM, on Las Vegas Boulevard, more commonly known as the Strip, where most of the more famous hotels in the city were aligned. There was Mandalay Bay, the Luxor, Excalibur, and New York–New York on one end; Circus Circus, the Riviera, the Sahara, and the Stratosphere on the other; and the Bellagio, Caesars Palace, Paris, and Bally's in between. So how could you go wrong?

Then there was the golf. Upon review of the available golf courses, we chose three venues that we thoroughly enjoyed. We played Bears Best (a Jack Nicklaus design), Angel Park (an Arnold Palmer design and another magnificent golf venue, which includes three courses, the Mountain being my favorite), and last but certainly not least we played Bali Hai, which is next to Mandalay Bay, right on the Strip.

Jack Nicklaus designed his Bears Best course by utilizing the signature golf hole layouts of some of his other outstanding golf course accomplishments to date and reproducing them in the Las Vegas landscape. The lush green fairways, which sharply contrasted the desert mountains and sand dunes in the background, were a breathtaking sight, especially if you have never been in the desert before.

Angel Park was also very enjoyable. There was a magnificent view of the golf course and a real green miniature golf course, the only one I had ever seen, right off the dining veranda and the clubhouse. It was a great setting for lunch as we took in the gorgeous panoramic view. Bali Hai was as exotic as the name exudes. With well over two thousand palm trees imported by the course designers, and the many thousands of other varied forms of exotic plant life, all of which were complemented by the beautiful white sand bunkers, this unique design added a tropical touch of the South Pacific to the desert, a unique and fun innovation to say the least. After thirty-six holes of golf at Bali Hai, my birthday celebration meal was a real treat. Dinner was at the elegant Wolfgang Puck Cili restaurant located right on the premises in the clubhouse at the Bali Hai golf course. The design and the ambiance of the restaurant and clubhouse were a continuation of the tropical theme so blatantly displayed on the golf course. During dinner we enjoyed their excellent cuisine, fine wine, dessert, and espresso with a touch of Sambuca, which topped off the meal. We also enjoyed some live piano music playing in the background that was the icing on my birthday cake, so to speak. After our dining experience at Cili, we headed to the casinos. New York City is known as the city that never sleeps, but Las Vegas is the literal personification of that expression. We walked from one end of the Strip to the other, stopping at almost every well-known casino in town, and all the joints were hopping no matter what time we went in. New York–New York, MGM, the Bellagio, Caesars, Bally's, and Paris were our favorite stops. I actually won a few grand at the Bellagio but gave it right back at the Paris. But you only live once, or do you?—a topic for another time. Having fun should be the priority. Remember, it's only money. Once you become enamored with the casino atmosphere lack of daylight and get into a hot run on the blackjack or craps tables, it is very easy to transpose night and day. The hours pass quickly. I see many people having dinner at 5:00 or 6:00 am and breakfast at 10:00 pm, or midnight for that matter. Since we were playing golf, we usually went to sleep around midnight and were out and about by 5:00 am or so the next morning, which is when we noted the varied dining habits of the habitual gamblers and nighttime crowd.

As we strolled down the Vegas Strip, I could almost feel the presence of some of the larger-than-life personalities who frequented Las Vegas in the fifties, sixties, and seventies, most notably Frank Sinatra, Dean Martin, Sammy Davis Jr., and the rest of the Rat Pack, to name a few. I was especially reminded of Frank Sinatra because Frank Junior's face was plastered on the big screen video monitor. He was singing all of his dad's hits and doing a pretty good job of it at that. Wayne Newton has been a lifer in Vegas and is still as popular as ever. Las Vegas has perhaps the biggest lineup of top-notch entertainment in the world. Wayne Newton, Barbra Streisand, Elton John, the Rolling Stones, Celine Dion, Tony Bennett, and the Blue Man Group, plus the first-class magic acts and much more, all entertain in Las Vegas. The list of famous Las Vegas personalities from the Golden Age would not be complete without including mention of perhaps the most well-known and idolized entertainer of all time—Mr. Las Vegas himself, the veritable King of Rock and Roll, Elvis Presley. His name is synonymous with the hierarchy of Las Vegas royalty, as they don't refer to him as the King for nothing. The list goes on and on. Just check online if you are planning a visit and you will note a dozen or more top- rated shows at any particular time. On our next night we walked the entire Strip again, beginning at Mandalay Bay and finishing at the Stratosphere. We stopped in at least six casinos, including MGM, New York–New York, Paris, Bally's, and the Bellagio. The lights were incredible and the water light show in front of the Bellagio was most enjoyable and entertaining. It also kept us out of the casinos for a while longer and saved me some dough, which made the time spent there that much more rewarding.

We revisited Las Vegas about four months later and got some great deals on golf and hotel rooms. I guess they figured they should lower the rates for anyone crazy enough to play golf in 114-degree temperatures.

It was tough, I must say, but we played and still had a good time, wet face cloths and all. It was another wonderful vacation under our belt, and they just keep getting better. If you're considering Las Vegas for your next trip, I can guarantee you won't be bored. It truly is the city that never sleeps.

You can get some terrific packages for both golf or just to stay and play at the resorts. Las Vegas is truly the ultimate playground for the over–twenty-one crowd. Happy vacationing and golfing to all!

Scottsdale, Arizona: The Myrtle Beach of the Southwest, Without the Beach

I have been traveling to Myrtle Beach since 1990 for great golf vacations and for the last four years with my golf buddies Ferd, Fred, Tim, Dennis, Richard, Peter, and Mike F. on our annual golf trip. Since this was to be our fifth year, we decided to try a new venue. After careful review of a number of alternate locations, we arrived at Scottsdale, Arizona, as this year's golf destination. It turned out to be an excellent choice, and we reserved our time there from March 18 to March 22. We were hoping for reasonable weather, as the week before we arrived the temperatures were in the high seventies, which is perfect for golf. When we arrived, the temperature rose into the high eighties and low nineties, which is hot but still playable. It is a drier climate, so the heat was not as formidable as in the North or Southeast, where the humidity makes it feel much warmer than it is.

The courses we played were TPC of Scottsdale, Las Sendas, Gold Canyon–Dinosaur, Whirlwind–Devil's Claw, and We-Ko-Pa–Cholla, my personal favorite. The rates at that time of the year were a little pricey but well worth the cost in retrospect. The last three golf resorts had thirty-six holes each, and we were able to replay another eighteen holes on their alternate course, which was most enjoyable and convenient. I have played desert golf previously in Las Vegas in 2002, as I vacationed there with my significant other that year to celebrate my fiftieth birthday, but this was different. The red rock mountains and varied rock and cactus formations and shapes were incredible. The green fairway grass against the colorful mountain backdrops was breathtaking. I enjoyed every minute of the trip. We stayed at the Xona Resort Suites, which was centrally located and had excellent accommodations for a reasonable price.

The elevation changes on Gold Canyon's Dinosaur course were most incredible, and the views from some of the higher altitudes were magnificent. After golf each day, the restaurant and nightlife scene was hopping.

We enjoyed Maggio's family-style restaurant, which offered so many pasta, fish, and meat specialties that it was hard to choose and at all-you- can-eat prices. We also enjoyed Capital Grill, another one of my favorites there. The only downside to this trip was the time of the flight from Newark, New Jersey, which was over five hours, and I was seated against the fuselage with no window. I always request a window seat when I travel because I enjoy taking pictures of the aerial views of the mountains, lakes, canyons, rivers, beautiful sunrise, sunsets, and sometimes even the cloud formations, so this seating arrangement was claustrophobic to say the least.

We normally go with a group of eight golfers, but this trip one of my good friends, Ferd, decided to invite a few acquaintances from San Francisco—Chris, Frank, and Dave. We also asked another associate from the Philadelphia area, Richard, to join us and round out the third foursome. There was some interesting golf banter and camaraderie between the new invitees and the former two foursomes. Everyone got along great, and the golf, good food, and good times were par for the course. As terrific a time as was had by all, I will still opt for Myrtle Beach as my first choice of golf venues. But Scottsdale, Arizona, is definitely a close second. If you are planning a golf trip or vacation, you cannot go wrong with either destination. The number of choices for excellent golf and accommodations at either venue is unlimited and includes many options for after-hours entertainment. For more information, you can check online at either myrtlebeachgolf.com or scottsdalegolf.com to find some information to help you start planning your golf trip. Have lots of fun, enjoy your trip, and happy golfing to all!

PART 4:

GOLF ON A BET–THE HOLE IN ONE AND FUN GAMES TO MAKE GOLF A LITTLE MORE INTERESTING

CHAPTER 12

THE HOLE IN ONE, OR ACE— NOT JUST A HIGH CARD IN A DECK

The ace may be a high playing card in a deck of cards, but it is also a most coveted prize in the game of golf. The ace, or proverbial hole in one, is considered an eagle on a par 3, which is the more common par for an ace or hole in one to occur. FYI, a birdie is the golf terminology for one under par, and an eagle is two strokes below par, either of which is a substantial accomplishment on any golf hole. On very rare occasions, a hole in one has also been recorded on par 4's, which is considered a double eagle and is 3 under par. This accomplishment is also known as an albatross, which it is called in the United Kingdom. On extremely rare occasions, a score of 1 has been recorded on par 5's. I'm assuming the score would be considered a triple eagle or double albatross. If there is an official name given for a hole in one on a par 5, I am not privy to it because of the extreme rarity of the occurrence. *Guinness World Records* notes a number of holes in one on par 5's, as does *Golf Digest* archives on occasion.

I can attest from personal experience that besides the skill factor, there is some luck involved in achieving a hole in one. I've been playing golf for over thirty years and have come so close to a hole in one on at least a dozen occasions. My ball has landed within twelve inches of the cup and within one half inch to six inches on at least six of those occasions. The reason I mentioned that some luck is involved is that one time I was playing with a relatively new golfer who was probably a 30 handicapper. His average score would normally be in the 105 range, and at the time I was a 12-handicap golfer. He hit his tee shot well off line on a par 3 hole of approximately 125 yards. The ball hit a tree, well off to the side of the hole, rebounded back onto the green, and went in the hole. I consider that pretty lucky. Would you agree? There are a number of other similar tales regarding holes in one, but most players who accomplish this feat are fairly skilled and usually play often.

One time while playing Marine Park Golf Course in Brooklyn, I was on the fourteenth hole par 5, which runs next to Flatbush Avenue. The hole is approximately 514 yards from the tee location we were playing that day. I hit a drive flush and launched it about 300 yards down the right side of the fairway. I was a fairly long hitter at the time, and I knew I could reach the green in 2 with a 5-iron for my second shot. I waited for the group in front to clear the green and hit another one on the screws, and I knew the ball was heading for the flag and the cup. The group in front was part of the Marine Park Golf Club, which I belonged to at the time. They were waving and cheering, so I thought the ball might have gone in. When I arrived at the green a few minutes later, the ball was sitting about a half inch from the cup and a double eagle. I had a tap in for an eagle, but a double eagle would have been much more rewarding for me than a hole in one because it is an even rarer feat to accomplish. I also came within a foot of a double eagle on a 275-yard par 4 one time, but once again it was not meant to be. My goal is to get that elusive ace before my sixtieth birthday, which is a few years away. I wish all you new and seasoned golfers alike the best of luck with achieving your hole in one.

CHAPTER 13

GOLF ON A BET: THE NASSAU— NOT JUST AN ISLAND IN THE BAHAMAS

One of the important but often overlooked aspects of golf is the terminology used in playing the game. Par, ace, bogie, double bogie, eagle, sandie, greenie, Nassau, etc., are all golf terms to be acquired while learning to play golf and will be addressed in another chapter. But what is "the Nassau"? you say. Well, I'm glad you asked. Nassau is not only a popular vacation destination in the Bahamas, but in terms of golf it is a friendly wager amongst friends to make the golf round a little more interesting. The term "Nassau," was derived from its creation at a country club in Nassau County, New York. In fact, it was the Nassau Country Club, which would make sense.

In my opinion, the Nassau is the most popular and fun format for betting in golf. It consists of a front nine-hole bet, a back nine bet, and an overall score bet that is determined by the team or individual player who has won the most holes in any particular golf round. As noted previously, the Nassau can be contested as an individual player or a team. There are also varied types of bets that can be made during a Nassau.

(**FORE Info:** I would be remiss if I didn't explain "handicap" here.

Just as in bowling, the handicap is the equalizer in competitive golf. In bowling a player gets spotted the difference between the average of another player that may be better than his. In other words, if player A has a 180 average and player B has a 150, player A has to give player B an 80, 90, or 100 percent spot, or 24, 27, or 30 pins respectively, depending on the rules established for a particular league or tournament, in order to equalize the fairness of any bet or competition. The same analysis applies to golf. If one player normally averages a score of 80, and some other golfer averages 95, then the 80 shooter will have to spot or handicap the other player with 15 shots, or a percentage of the difference in stroke average.)

The number of strokes will depend on the rules established by the club or tournament for that particular competition. Besides stroke play, which is the count of all the strokes incurred for the front nine, the back nine, and the overall score, you can play by match play, which is a hole-by-hole format whereby you have an individual game for each hole and the player with the most winning holes at the end of the first or front nine, the back nine, and the overall eighteen holes is declared the winner. In stroke play, the handicap is deducted from the total score at the end of the front nine, the back nine, and the overall score to determine the winner. In match play the handicap is adjusted on each hole. As you know, there are eighteen holes in professional golf, and each hole has a difficulty rating depending on its rank against the other holes on the golf course. Since there are eighteen holes, the holes will rank in difficulty from one through eighteen. If a player is entitled to fifteen strokes in stroke or match play, then he will receive a stroke on the fifteen most difficult holes on the golf course. (**FORE Info:** See the score card for the difficulty rank of each hole.)

The other three remaining holes will be played with no handicap, so the player receiving strokes should take advantage of the opportunity where they receive strokes whenever possible. There are many different formats that can be utilized when playing a Nassau, but the one I enjoy the most is low and overall, which keeps all players in the competition and can only be played with four players. This means that the player with the lowest score on any given hole would get one point and the total of both players on the team with the aggregate total lowest score would receive another point.

If the two low-scoring players tie on any hole, then no points would be received because the bet is cancelled out by each other's score. The same would go for the total score if the teams were even on that hole. The handicap of each player is considered on each hole and is added or deducted accordingly before a point is allowed for that hole.

A friendly bet is usually two to five dollars per front, back, and overall, which would mean a total loss of six to fifteen dollars if one team or player lost all three bets. The teams should be made so that they are as evenly matched as possible to allow for a fair and fun match. There is also an additional bet that can be added to the game called "the press." The press is a bet that can be automatic or at a player's discretion, depending on how many holes he or she is down and the player's optimism that he or she can beat the other player or team and win any lost money back. In automatic press format, if you are down by a hole you automatically have an additional bet on the next hole, and the potential loss or gain can become substantial using this format. For beginning golfers I recommend a simple two-dollar bet and optional presses after you have established somewhat of a handicap. To establish your handicap, you should average at least ten scores and use that average to establish how many strokes you give or take from the other player or players with whom you are competing.

As noted earlier, there are many fun betting formats in golf to make the game even more interesting, competitive, and enjoyable. Next time you're out playing with friends, give it a try, even if just for fun and no money is exchanged at the end. But remember to have an enjoyable time.

PART 5:

THE CHAMPIONS OF GOLF AND GOLF'S MOST PRESTIGIOUS TOURNAMENTS

CHAPTER 14

JACK NICKLAUS AND TIGER WOODS: THE BEST OF THE BEST

I mentioned Jack Nicklaus in the title first because alphabetically and historically I think he deserves that courtesy, but they should both be credited with phenomenal accomplishments for their time in golf history. I grew up with Jack Nicklaus as my golf hero, just as I had Mickey Mantle as my baseball idol in my formative years. I have admired many ball players since, but no one can take the place of Mantle in my book. There have been many great players both in his era and subsequently who may have been historically and statistically better than he, but he still remains my all-time favorite. As far as I am concerned, Mantle was the best and will always be the best, case closed. The same goes for Jack Nicklaus, as he will always be number one in my book. Tiger is a phenom, no two ways about it. It would have been a heck of a battle to see Tiger and Jack go head-to- head in their primes. It would be like Muhammad Ali vs. Rocky Marciano. Who was really the best? We'll never know for sure on either count, but our minds can play it out and choose whom we think would come out on top. I'm a big Tiger Woods fan, but Phil Mickelson is not far behind. Watching Jack's duels with Arnold Palmer (and I mention his name with all the respect it deserves), Tom Watson, Lee Trevino, Gary Player, Johnny Miller, and Tom Weiskopf was incomparable to the modern-day era of golf, at least in my book. I don't mean to take anything away from the modern- day PGA pro. Tiger Woods, Phil Mickelson, Vijay Singh, Jim Furyk, and more than a handful of other players, including Fred Couples and Davis Love III, whose ability with a golf club would allow them to be competitive in any era of golf, are all great players. It's just not the same game to me. Through no fault of their own, the equipment and golf ball technology and advancement accessible for the modern-day professional has made golf a different game than it was twenty years ago or more.

I was a youngster at the time other golfing greats, like Ben Hogan, Byron Nelson, Sam Snead, Bobby Jones, Gene Sarazen, and the like, were competing, but I can still watch some of their duels on *Shell's Wonderful World of Golf.* I often wondered how they would have fared in the modern- day era. These guys used wooden clubs and inferior golf balls and were still striping 250- to 280-yard drives down the middle of the fairway and shaping shots like it was second nature to them. My favorite is the duel between Byron Nelson and Ben Hogan at Pine Valley, New Jersey, the number-one rated course in the world. I'll leave it to your imagination to figure out who the winner was, but B. H. were his initials. When I was following Jack Nicklaus's career in my youth, I never imagined that anyone could ever match his record, let alone beat it. So many golfing greats had phenomenal records in their careers—Arnold, Gary, Tom, Ben, Sam, Byron, Bobby, and the rest—but he was well ahead of the pack. Tiger has shown the world what the power of the mind can do. His dad Earl helped him establish early in his childhood that if you want to be the best, you have to set that goal in your sights and contemplate on it every day and visualize yourself accomplishing that goal. It is public knowledge that Tiger had his sights set on Jack Nicklaus's record at a very early age. It was an unreachable goal for most because they would not let themselves believe that it was possible, but not for Tiger. That's what makes him stand out above the rest.

It is inevitable that Tiger will beat Jack's record, as long as he remains healthy, and I wish him well on his quest. After all, records are made to be broken. He is a remarkable player and I would like nothing more than to see him in action one day. My ideal foursome would be Jack Nicklaus, Arnold Palmer, Tiger (and I can say Tiger because he is more than a few years younger than me), and naturally me. What a day it would be. I can hit the ball fairly well and I always wondered how I would fare against the best. In my younger days at Marine Park or Marine Dunes Golf Course in Brooklyn, I hit the ball well and par 4's and 5's were usually within reach on my second shot, depending on wind conditions. I know it may never happen but I can dream, can't I? Dreams do come true, you know. If you have any doubts about what I say, ask Mr. Walt Disney or Tiger Woods if they believe, and I'm pretty sure we both know what their answer would be.

So, whatever your goals in life may be—to beat Jack's or Tiger's record, Jordan or Kobe in basketball, Marciano, Ali, or Roy Jones in boxing, Montana, Marino or Brady in football, or whatever other achievement you may be striving to accomplish—take a tip from Nike: Just do it.

CHAPTER 15

THE MAJOR GOLF
TOURNAMENTS

The Masters: April 2009—What Might Have Been?

The winner of the Masters this past April, Angel Cabrera, ultimately deserved the title of Masters champion. Having been in contention with his stellar play the first three rounds and playing steadily on the earlier holes on Sunday, he was all but out of the running a few holes later when he dropped from –12 to –9 with bogies. He never conceded to the competition and rallied back to –12 under and seized every opportunity to stay in the game by making birdies when he needed to. It only goes to enforce the old adage that slow and steady wins the race. Even after he tied with Chad Campbell and Kenny Perry for a playoff, he all but stymied himself when he hit behind a tree on the first playoff hole on number eighteen. Chad Campbell and Kenny Perry were in the fairway in great shape, but Masters Sunday nerves got the better of them. They both pushed what would normally be routine iron shots into the green to the right and left, leaving the door open for Angel. He seized the moment by first making a lucky punch draw shot that hit a tree and caromed into the fairway, leaving him a clear shot to the green. He capitalized on that opportunity by executing an excellent lob wedge shot in an extreme pressure situation. He landed on the green in 3 with an approximate 12-foot putt, which he converted to tie Kenny Perry's par save, and went on to the next playoff hole. Chad was not as lucky and was unable to salvage par, so it left Kenny Perry and his playing partner, Angel Cabrera, all day to duke it out once again. This time it was on the tenth hole, which turned out to be the deciding hole of the Masters. Kenny hit his tee shot into the left trap while Angel hit safely down the middle of the fairway since he wasn't going to make the same mistake he made previously on number eighteen. His second shot was safely on the green while Kenny had yanked his left out of the fairway trap, leaving himself with a very tough approach shot to get close enough to save par, which he needed to keep his Masters hopes alive.

He left himself about a twenty-five–foot putt and missed just short on the right while Angel easily converted his two putt for par and victory. Congratulations to Angel on his amazing victory, but I must admit I was disappointed by the way things played out.

Had I scripted this Masters, it would have gone something like this. Tiger Woods and Phil Mickelson had teed off earlier and both started at –4. Phil's rally on the front nine was reminiscent of the Nicklaus charge in the '86 Masters, my favorite Masters to date. This year's Masters was a close second but anticlimactic because Phil Mickelson, Tiger Woods, and Kenny Perry were not victorious in the end. When Phil turned the front in 30 or –10, I thought to myself that this was far from over and could be one of the greatest Masters ever. Since I had tuned in when Phil and Tiger first teed off, to the finale, I could not take my eyes off the TV screen. The steady and stellar play by Angel, Kenny, Tiger, and Phil was riveting. The two best players in the world were going head-to-head and catching the leaders after having been seven shots back when they first teed off on Sunday morning. After Phil's 30 on the front nine holes I knew Tiger had to make his move if he wanted to catch Phil, who was now at –10. He accomplished this by eagling the thirteenth hole subsequent to Phil's double bogie on hole twelve when he made a mental error by not using enough club to carry over Rae's creek and land on a safe part of the green. Tiger and Phil still both had an opportunity, but they also missed possible eagle opportunities on the fifteenth, which left them with more work ahead if they were to taste victory. Phil and Tiger had at one point reached –11 and –10, respectively, and were both standing at victory's doorstep when they faltered at the end. Tiger bogied the last two holes in un-Tigerlike fashion, and Phil did not do much better. When they both came up short at eighteen, I was hoping that Kenny Perry, who had been playing some of the best golf of his life for the past two years or more, could become the oldest player at forty-eight years to win the Masters. His –14 standing at the end of the sixteenth hole had all but sewed it up. A par on one of the last two holes would have clinched victory for him. He had not gotten a bogie for the previous twenty-two holes, so why start now? But start now he did with two consecutive bogies to finish at –12 tied with Cabrera and Campbell. The playoff loomed.

Kenny's steady play had come to an end, and the pressure of Masters Sunday finally got the better of him. He all but handed the victory to Angel, who appeared more relaxed than the others and just happy to be there in contention without succumbing as much to the pressures of the day.

As we know, Angel Cabrera wins, but it would have been something if Tiger, Phil, and Kenny had tied for a playoff on that fateful Sunday Masters afternoon. I guess we'll never know the outcome, but it sure is nice to ponder a Masters playoff scenario that very nearly was.

The Rain Man, Glover, Captures U.S. Open Title at Bethpage Black 2009

The U.S. Open returned to the Bethpage Black Course in June, 2009 on Long Island, New York, where it last decimated the field leaving Tiger Woods as the only player standing and below par in 2002. Its fearful reputation was softened a bit by the steady rainfall during this year's tournament. But make no mistake about it, many players were still well over par and missed the cut by making the error of missing the fairway on critical holes.

As with the Masters, I have to admit I am disappointed in the outcome of this year's Open. With wife Amy awaiting surgery, and her request for a win, I thought surely Phil would pull this one out of the hat. He is as capable as any and more so than most when it comes to golf skills, but the majors still seem to elude him when he is in contention on Sunday. When he made his move and went to –4, he appeared psyched. I thought this would surely be the one, a real Cinderella story in the making, but it was not destined to be. He missed a three-foot putt on the fifteenth hole and a makeable par putt on the seventeenth that ended his chances for his and Amy's dream finish. Bethpage Black reared its ugly head and clutched victory away from not only Phil Mickelson, but also Ricky Barnes and another Cinderella story contender in David Duval. They all finished tied at –2 and with a share of the second-place prize. David Duval looked a bit heavier since his stellar play around the turn of the century. At that time he was ranked second in the world behind none other than Tiger Woods, and David had played well during this Open. Second behind Tiger was not a bad place to be at that time, but he has struggled over the past four or five years and has missed quite a few cuts. He finally recaptured some of the form at Bethpage Black that made him one of the top players in the world at that time in his career. The U.S. amateur champion in 2002, Ricky Barnes, dropped six shots in his last round and just missed birdie at eighteen. A birdie would have put a little pressure on Lucas Glover but the putt slid by on the left side, which ended any chance for a tie and a playoff. Lucas two putted easily for par and victory. Lucas Glover, a really good player with all the skills needed to win, remained the most calm out of the final players on Monday. Neither Bethpage Black nor any of the other contenders could take the prize away from him. He did drop three shots in the final round, but the Rain Man, Glover, played intelligently enough to outlast the competition.

Tiger Woods played well and also made a run at the title but came up short this time. I can see a marked improvement in his game, since surgery, but even Tiger needs time to work his way back into true form after the knee surgery sidelined him for almost nine months. Congratulations to Lucas Glover for his tremendous victory in this year's U.S. Open under adverse conditions and an extremely tough venue to test one's golf skills, Bethpage Black. Next, the British Open.

The British Open 2009: Tom Watson—A Golfer for the Ages

The British Open was the third major of the year that did not end the way I would have scripted it. The Masters had an improbable winner in Angel Cabrera when Tiger Woods and Phil Mickelson were in the hunt and let it slip away on the last few holes. Kenny Perry, then forty-eight years old, had it all sewed up until the last two holes, which he bogied, and opened the door for Angel to win in a playoff. In the second major of the year, the U.S. Open winner could have easily been Phil Mickelson, who was playing his heart out for his ailing wife, Amy, but he could not hold onto the lead on Sunday and lost out to Lucas Glover. Now Tom Watson, one of the greatest golfers and British Open champions who ever lived, lost to Stewart Cink in a playoff that didn't have to be.

Tom Watson had given the fans so many thrills all week, and after the first round, even though tied for the lead, most of the golf authoritarians had already written him off and said he had virtually no chance for victory. Tom Watson had other ideas, and I was rooting for him all the way.

He kept coming back, and even after four bogies in a row during one of the rounds, he bounced back with birdies and pars when he needed to and fought his way back into the lead. His play was reminiscent of the Tom Watson I so fondly remembered in his prime in the seventies. At this very venue in 1977 he faced down Jack Nicklaus, the greatest golfer who ever lived, for the final thirty-six holes and beat him by a shot.

After having given a valiant effort for all four rounds, the eighteenth hole of the final round turned out to be the defining hole of the tournament. Tom Watson was leading by two shots going into the eighteenth hole, and a par would have clinched it for him. But again at the British Open the improbable happened. Stewart Cink birdied the hole and Tom bogied to force a playoff. Tom hit his 8-iron approach shot to the eighteenth green flush and got a bad break when it hit on the green and, instead of checking up, it rolled off the back and left him with an uphill shot back to the green. He opted for the putter, which had served him well all week, but he hit it a bit too hard to get through the fringe and went past the cup by about eight to ten feet. The putt coming back was makeable, but he hit it short and missed to the right. Had he sunk that putt, the Open title would have been his and golf history would have been made. He may have lost the Claret Jug but he is a winner in my book.

I noted previously that the improbable happened when Tom lost on the eighteenth hole. That statement is not true, because in reality, he lost in a four-hole playoff to Cink after tying on the eighteenth hole. Tom had been playing so well for the first seventy-one holes that when he didn't get the result he anticipated after hitting a very well-struck 8-iron for his approach shot to the eighteenth green, it appeared to knock the wind out of his sails. He seemed to have lost on eighteen rather than in the playoff, and it appeared that he may have finally had enough. In retrospect, the improbable is the fact that the fifty-nine-year-old Watson was competing on a level never before seen in a major by a golfer his age, against the best players in the world, for four pressure-packed days, on a very tough golf course under extreme conditions. It would have been an awesome feat for Tom Watson to have been victorious and to clinch his sixth British Open title, but he will always be a champion in my book.

He came very close to victory, and for those naysayers who thought he did not have a chance, I hope they now realize that if you have the heart and belief in yourself, as Tom Watson did, all things are possible. After Tom Watson's performance in this year's British Open, I would not be surprised if next year Jack, Arnie, Gary, and Tom go head-to-head like old times. In closing I would like Tom Watson to know he will always be remembered as one helluva golfer not only by his peers but by all of us. Thank you, Tom, for making believers out of us!

Congratulations to Stewart Cink for his victory and some

extraordinary play against the field and one of the world's best golfers and gentleman, Tom Watson.

The 91st PGA Championship at Hazeltine National Golf Club in Chaska, Minnesota: Tiger's Wire-to- Wire PGA Victory Gets Short-circuited by Yang!

Tiger Woods has been victorious in fourteen out of fourteen attempts in the major championships when leading or sharing the lead after fifty-four holes. Tiger's game has been sharp over the last few weeks, including back-to-back victories in the fifty-first and final playing of the Buick Open, which he has dominated so brilliantly over the years, and also the WGC–Bridgestone Invitational at Firestone Country Club in Akron, Ohio. He beat the field handily by three and four strokes, respectively, thus dispelling any doubts about his return to true Tiger form.

Yang also made some noise and came in alone in fifth place at the Buick, tied for nineteenth at Firestone, and has played well as of late. He ranked 110 in the world until his PGA win, which should put him well ahead of that number.

I must take a moment to ask, What happened to Padraig Harrington? Having started the day at –6 and in excellent position to make a run at the title, he dropped off the leader board and shot 78 to put himself out of the running for back-to-back titles and another Wanamaker Trophy. It makes me seriously wonder whether Padraig would have been victorious in last year's two final majors, the British Open and the PGA, since he has faltered in both the Buick Open and the 2009 PGA when Tiger Woods was in the field. It may be the intimidation factor that exudes with Woods's mere presence, which could affect Padraig Harrington's performance when going head-to-head with Tiger. There are many affected players, but it did not seem to bother P. E. Yang on the back nine on Sunday or, for that matter, at any time in the final round. He played well throughout the round, and his only hiccup came on 17 when he three-putted for bogie and left the door open for Tiger. Tiger pulled his approach shot left and into the rough just off the green. His attempt to chip out left him short, and he could not convert the par putt to return to -7 and a tie with Yang going into the final hole. I guess you could say he did not Wan-a-maker (a little play on words there). Yang's second shot on 18 was a hybrid over the trees, which landed on the green and left him in good position to par or even birdie the hole. Tiger needed to hit his approach shot stiff if he was to have any chance for victory. Instead, he overshot the green and again left himself with a difficult shot from the rough to birdie or even par the hole, which he ultimately failed to do. Tiger had to settle for bogie to Yang's birdie leaving him an unprecedented three shots back at -5. Yang finished at -8, where Tiger had started for the day.

When Tiger was ahead by two shots at the turn, I said to myself, "This PGA is over," but Yang had other ideas. P. E. Yang played well, no two ways about it. It seemed that Tiger uncharacteristically changed his strategy mid-round to a more conservative approach, which is atypical for him.

He appeared to be protecting his two-stroke lead instead of his normal aggressive style and using his unequivocal ability to expand that lead to three, four, or even five strokes. Tiger did not appear to trust his game as he laid up on a number of holes. He left himself much longer approach shots than Yang, and this tactic may have ultimately lent itself to his demise and loss of the championship.

I know the missed cut at the British Open did not sit well with Tiger, and I'm sure he worked even harder with his coach, Hank Haney, to correct any swing faults in preparation for the PGA Championship. Second place is not a bad spot to be in but unacceptable by Tiger's standards. I'm sure he would have much rather had today's headline read "Tiger Wins Wire- to-Wire Victory in PGA Championship" or "Tiger Wins 15th Major" or "Tiger Edges Closer to Jack Nicklaus's Record 18 Majors and Sam Snead's All-Time 82 Victory Record," but it was not to be this time. It just goes to show that even the infallible Tiger Woods is human and can lose when the chips do not fall in his direction. This is the fourth straight major with an unlikely victor accepting the trophy. In the Masters, Angel Cabrera held off late charges by Tiger Woods and Phil Mickelson, who blew opportunities on the final nine on Sunday, and Chad Campbell and Kenny Perry, who had it sewed up at the sixteenth until he bogied both finishing holes to force a playoff in which he lost to Angel. At the U.S. Open, Phil Mickelson was once again in contention on Sunday and playing his heart out for wife Amy who had requested him to win. David Duval and Ricky Barnes, who could not hold on to a six-stroke lead, allowed Lucas Glover to snatch victory right out from under them. Then, there was an unprecedented performance in the British Open by Tom Watson, who easily could have won, but Stewart Cink tied him on the eighteenth and handily beat him in the playoff that ensued. Finally, in the PGA—what can I say—Tiger Woods is beaten by P. E. Yang on the back nine on Sunday. Who could have imagined a more implausible ending to the last major of the season, given Tiger's two-stroke lead at the turn? This is when Tiger usually makes his move and can catch an opponent with a four-stroke lead or more when he turns it on. A Tiger Woods major victory was not in the cards in 2009, and his continuing quest toward Jack Nicklaus's record will have to wait until a future date.

Please note that Tiger's 2009 season had been very successful, as he was the leading money winner, the leader in the FedEx and Presidents Cup standings, not to mention his longstanding status as number one in the world ranking, which remains intact. His next opportunity will come in the FedEx Cup where he can add another victory and move closer to Sam Snead's all-time victory total of eighty-two. Not too shabby from a player who is still somewhat recovering from his ACL knee surgery in 2008.

Congratulations to P. E. Yang for his victory in the 91st PGA Championship and his stellar play over all four rounds, especially on the back nine on Sunday against the world's best player, Tiger Woods.

PART 6:

GOLF 'S CHAMPIONS AND GOLF TERMINOLOGY–A MUST FOR THE BEGINNING GOLFER

CHAPTER 16

TOP TWENTY ALL-TIME BEST

All-Time Greatest Male Golfers

1. Jack Nicklaus
2. Tiger Woods
3. Bobby Jones
4. Ben Hogan
5. Sam Snead
6. Arnold Palmer
7. Byron Nelson
8. Gary Player
9. Walter Hagen
10. Tom Watson
11. Harry Vardon
12. Young Tom Morris
13. Seve Ballesteros
14. Gene Sarazen
15. Lee Trevino
16. Old Tom Morris
17. Billy Casper

All-Time Greatest Female Golfers

1. Mickey Wright (number 8, rank in the top 20)
2. Annika Sorenstam (number 12)
3. Babe Zaharias (number 16)

*as listed in *Golf Magazine* 50th Anniversary Issue September 2009

Top Ten List of All-Time Favorite Golfers

1. Jack Nicklaus—always will be my favorite, and deservingly so.
2. Tiger Woods—a close second, a phenomenal player, and by far the best golfer in the modern era.
3. Ben Hogan—from 1946 to1953 the best golfer in the world. His swing technique and form were some of the greatest ever.
4. Arnold Palmer—"The King." Although he may not have the most majors or wins, he was the royalty of the modern era of golf and is still the greatest. "Arnie's Army" can attest to that.
5. Bobby Jones—from 1923 to 1930 the best in the world. If he had not retired so soon, maybe the greatest player ever. I think the thirteen majors won in a seven-year stretch speaks for itself.
6. Tom Watson—His rivalry with Jack Nicklaus will go down in the annals of golf history. His performance in the 2009 British Open at fifty-nine years of age solidifies his name as one of the greatest golfers ever. He will always be remembered as one helluva golfer.
7. Gary Player—a great player and tough competitor. Just ask Jack, Arnold, and Tom. From the late fifties to late seventies, he gave them all a run for their money. Still going strong on the senior tour.
8. Phil Mickelson—a golfer with all the tools who could be one of the greatest ever. Needs to take it to the next level, especially in the majors. Great guy with a lot of heart and right on top in my book.

9. Sam Snead—awesome player with the most golf tournament wins ever. Not so much in the majors but great just the same.

10. Byron Nelson—His record of eleven in a row and eighteen total victories in 1945 may never be equaled. Good Luck, Tiger, with this one! This record is in line with breaking Joe DiMaggio's fifty- six–game hitting streak.

Honorable Mention

A few more top golfers too good not to mention are:

1. Lee Trevino—could do anything with a golf ball. Gave Jack a run for the money on a few occasions and can give Tiger some competition with his golf tricks.

2. Johnny Miller—Another great player in his prime, a bit streaky, but watch out when he is on a run.

3. Fred Couples—I just like the guy, and he is another player who could have achieved greatness had it not been for his injuries.

4. Seve Ballesteros—can go head-to-head with Tiger when it comes to making a golf ball do what he wants it to. A great and exciting career. He is as courageous in his battle with his illness as he was on the golf course. The best of luck, Seve!

CHAPTER 17

A GLOSSARY OF GOLF
TERMS AND DEFINITIONS

It is good for the beginning golfer to learn some of the more widely used terminology associated with golf. It will also help you to better understand how to play the game. Included below is an alphabetical list of some of the terms that you should get to know while learning to play. They are as follows:

Ace: A hole in one or eagle on a par 3. (See Chapter 12, The Hole in One, or Ace—Not Just a High Card in a Deck, for elaboration on the term "ace" in golf.)

Albatross: A term more widely used and originating in the United Kingdom. It is another name for a double eagle, or 3 below par on a golf hole. Extremely rare and can only be achieved on par 4's or higher.

Ball Markers: A marker, usually round in shape, used to mark the spot on the green where your golf ball has landed and may be obstructing the putting line to the golf hole of another player in your group, another rule of golf etiquette.

Ball Retriever: A telescoping device used to retrieve golf balls that can be stored in your golf bag. This device will allow you to retrieve a ball that lands in a water hazard, over a fence, or in an otherwise inaccessible location.

Ball Washer: The ball washer is usually placed adjacent the tee box, or right on the golf cart itself, to allow you to wash the mud and dirt off your golf ball after playing the previous hole. It is good practice to use the washer when necessary because the dirt can affect the ball flight and distance achieved.

Birdie: One below par, or a score of two on a par 3, three on a par 4, four on a par 5, etc.

Bogie: One over par, or four on a par 3, five on a par 4, six on a par 5, etc.

Bunker: Another name for a sand trap (see Sand Trap). Sometimes a bit deeper than a normal sand trap would be.

Cup: The plastic or metal cup-shaped device cut and placed in the green at an area where the flagstick will be placed for a particular golf hole. (FORE **Info:** The cup diameter is approximately three times the diameter of the golf ball, or four and a quarter inches. Why is the diameter of the golf cup four and a quarter inches? The diameter of the golf cup evolved purely by chance. Two golfers on the St. Andrews links found that one hole was so badly worn that they could not use it. Much of its sand had been removed by previous players for building tees. Anxious to repair the damage and continue their game, they looked around and discovered nearby part of an old drainpipe. They inserted this in the hole. It was the first "cup," and because it happened to measure four and a quarter inches across, all cups are now that size.)

Divot: A clump of grass removed from the fairway or other location on the course caused by the descending path of the player's club after the golf ball is struck. A divot is also an indentation on the green caused when a golf ball lands.

Divot Repair or Replacement: An important rule of golf and etiquette is to repair or replace all divots made while playing golf. It is a courtesy to the next player who lands in that area so that the grass is repaired and ready for him to have the same opportunity as the golfer did when he hit the shot prior. If the actual divot or clump of grass cannot be replaced, then at least an effort has been made to do so. Also on many courses, because of the different types of grasses used for varied climates and sustenance, a mixture of seed and fertilizer is used in lieu of the actual replacement of the divot. Be sure to observe these local rules and courtesies for you and your fellow players.

Divot Repair Tool: A pronged tool used to repair the indentation in the green caused by a golf ball landing on any area of said green.

Double Bogie: A score of two over par, or a five on a par 3, six on a par 4, 7 on a par 5, etc.. A **Triple Bogie** would be three over par, a **Quadruple Bogie** is four over par, etc.

Double Eagle (aka **Albatross,** see definition above): Three below par, or a hole in one on a par 4, a two on a par 5, a three on a par 6, etc. It is a rare feat and accomplishment in golf.

Draw: The travel path of the golf ball from right to left (for right-handed golfers, and opposite for left-handed golfers). (**FORE Info:** The golf professional adjusts both grip and setup to allow for a deliberate draw of the golf ball, which also promotes more distance when it lands.)

Driver: The club with the least amount of loft and the largest head. Drivers normally vary from 6 to 10.5 degrees, and the shafts measure from 43 to 45 inches in length and are meant to be used to drive the ball and attain the maximum distance on the longer golf holes.

Eagle: Two below par, or a hole in one on a par 3, two on a par 4, three on a par 5, etc.

Etiquette: Etiquette is defined in the dictionary as "any special code of behavior or courtesy." In golf there are many courtesies to be extended to both the golf course and your fellow golfers. See Chapter 1 regarding golf etiquette for more information.

Fade: The path of the golf ball flight from left to right (again, for the right-handed golfer, and the opposite for the left-handed golfer). (**FORE:** The golf professional adjusts both grip and setup to allow for this type of deliberate ball flight.)

Flagstick: The pole with a flag attached, which is placed in the cup on the green, to designate the location of the cup or hole on each golf hole.

Fore: A term used to warn others on a golf course when an errant shot may be heading their way. It should be yelled loudly enough so that the player or players can hear if the ball may be heading in their direction.

Foursome: A name associated with a group of four golfers, which is the maximum standard number of players allowed in any golf group.

Golf: The name given to this wonderful game and whose derivation was explained as follows: **G** stands for Gentleman, **O** stands for Only, **L** stands for Ladies, and **F** stands for Forbidden, so together it would read "Gentleman Only Ladies Forbidden." I cannot attest for sure if this was the actual derivation of the name, but refer to Chapter 1 on golf etiquette for more information.

Golf Bag: A bag with compartments used to store and carry your golf clubs, balls, and accessories during a golf round.

Golf Ball: A dimpled ball used to play the game of golf. The diameter of a regulation golf ball is 1.68 inches. (Note: A minimum of 1.68 inches. The old British 1.62-inch standard became obsolete in 1990.)

Golf Cart: A player has two options to traverse the golf course. One is to walk and the other is to ride in a cart. I enjoy walking, but many of the newer resort courses are designed with the holes so far apart that walking is discouraged and near impossible in some cases. It is also so that the owners will receive the additional revenue from the golf cart rental. Some courses do allow walking, and the walking carts are about three to six dollars to rent. There are also lightweight carry bags that can be used, but I would not recommend them on a hot summer day or on a course with very hilly terrain. You can make the choice of your personal preference as you learn to play and acquire more experience, but I suggest an electric or motorized gas cart when you are first learning to play. It will help keep up the pace of play and allow the beginning golfer to observe one of the important rules of golf etiquette.

Golfer: A person who plays golf.

Hazard: An area usually marked by red stakes and in which the golf club cannot be grounded if one lands in this location. If the ball is located and is playable, then the golfer should observe the same rules about the grounding of the golf club as if he or she had landed in a sand trap. If the ball is lost, the player should take a drop along the line of the golf ball as it entered the hazard and assess a one-stroke penalty at the end of the hole.

Hole in One: A score of one, or an ace or eagle on a par 3. It signifies that only one golf shot was required to get the golf ball into the cup on the green. (**FORE Info:** Holes in one have been made and recorded on par 4's, aka double eagles. They have also been recorded on extremely rare occasions on par 5's, which would be a triple eagle or double albatross. See the *Guinness World Records* and *Golf Digest* for more information.)

Iron: The term used for the clubs with flat metal heads used in golf. The 1-iron through the 9-iron are the standard numbered irons manufactured. A golf club set may include a 10-iron. (See Chapter 13 for more info.)

Out of Bounds or OB: An area usually marked by white stakes and running parallel to a golf hole. If a golf ball lands on the opposite side of the aforementioned stakes, the player who hit the ball loses stroke and distance and must re-hit again from the tee or wherever he was playing from when the ball went out of bounds. (**FORE Info:** If hitting from the tee area, the player will re-tee and be hitting three, or what would be considered the third shot. If he is unfortunate enough to hit out of bounds again, his next shot would be his fifth. If hitting from the fairway, he would be hitting two over the number of strokes played to the point where the ball went out of bounds.) (**FORE Warning:** Try to hit away from the out-of-bounds areas and align yourself with an area toward the opposite side of the fairway where you will have more room for a safe golf shot.)

Par: The number of strokes designated for a particular golf hole. Golf courses are designed to include par 3's, par 4's, and par 5's, and the total strokes allowed for eighteen holes is usually seventy-two. Most regulation golf courses consist of four par 3's, ten par 4's, and four par 5's. There are also par 6's on some courses, such as Farmstead, which is located in both North and South Carolina, just north of Myrtle Beach. The hole plays from approximately 760 yards from the championship tees. During one golf round that I played there, I just missed an eagle 4 by two inches with a putt from the fringe of the green and played from the 716-yard tee location. I made the tap-in birdie but the hole in one and double eagle still elude me. There are also par 70 and 71 courses, and they can consist of a combination of the above-referenced par holes.

Pin: Another name for the flagstick but not as widely used or accepted any longer.

Provisional Shot: A secondary golf ball which is played after you have just hit your shot and are not sure if it went out of bounds or in a water hazard, woods, or any area where it may not be retrievable or playable without penalty, etc. If you find your original ball in bounds, no penalty is assessed. If you have to play the provisional ball, a one-stroke penalty must be added to your total score at the end of the golf hole.

Putt or **Putting:** The name of the stroke used for the golf shot associated with rolling the ball on the green toward the cup or flagstick. The golf ball is usually struck with a putter on the green, but any club can be used for this shot.

Putter: The club used for putting to the golf cup or flagstick from on or off the green.

Pronate: To turn one's hands and forearms over to the left or right, depending on whether a player is right- or left-handed, respectively, when starting the follow-through or finish part of the golf swing.

Replay: Most golf courses offer a special rate to play an additional nine or eighteen holes after you have completed your initial eighteen hole golf round. This option is known as a replay. The prices are about half of the original green fee rate and any golfer who would like to continue to play should take advantage of this reduction in price. When I am on vacation I always replay because I enjoy the game and the lower pricing makes it that much better. Some golf courses even offer a replay for cart fees only, which is usually about $20 to $25 which is an excellent deal.

Sand Trap: A strategic placement of sand usually around the green or next to the fairway in the driving zones to make scoring more of a challenge for the golfer.

Sandie: A term given to achieving a score of par after having landed in a greenside bunker or sand trap.

Single: One person arriving at the course to play golf.

Snowman: A score of 8 on a golf hole. The name was derived because the number 8 is shaped somewhat like a snowman. I think his head may be missing?

Tee: The wooden or plastic device used to tee the golf ball on the tee box on each hole. (**FORE Info:** Tees come in varied lengths, 2 1/8", 2 3/4", and 3 1/4" being the most common. Be sure to select the proper tee length for the club being used. See the Equipment section in Chapter 1 for more info.)

Tee Box: The area at each hole designated for the first shot to be hit from that particular golf hole. (**FORE:** The golf courses are designed with different tee box locations on each hole, set up for the different skill levels of the golfer. Make sure to select the tee box that is appropriate for your level of play. Beginning golfers usually play from the white markers or around 5,800 to 6,300 yards long for the men, and the red markers varying from 4500 to 5200 yards for women. If you are finding that these tee boxes are not challenging enough, you can select a tee location farther back. I do not think this will be the case when you first learn to play.)

Tee Markers: The markers placed at the tee box on each hole signifying where to tee your ball. (**FORE Warning:** Do not tee the golf ball forward of this area closer to the golf hole, a rule of golf and golf etiquette.)

Threesome: A group of three players on the golf course playing together. They may also be paired with a single player if the starter or course play dictates.

Twosome: Two players who are scheduled to play together on the golf course. They can be paired with another single or two other players or can play as a twosome if course conditions permit.

Woods: The name given to the clubs that used to be manufactured in wood—persimmon being the most common. The 2-wood, 3- wood, 4-wood, 5-wood, 7-wood, and so on are all now made in the newest and most technologically advanced metal products. (**FORE Warning:** Not to be confused with Tiger Woods, who is the most gifted golf athlete on the planet.)

EPILOGUE

I've thoroughly enjoyed the time I spent in preparing this guide for the beginning golfer. As noted previously, I wish that I had the information included in these pages when I was first learning to play. The most important piece of advice or information that I could impart to the reader is to make the most of your time on the golf course and never allow the frustrations that can be experienced while playing golf detract from the benefits and pleasures that can be derived from doing so.

Another very important experience to be gained from playing golf, which took me many years to realize, is to enjoy the collateral benefits associated with playing the game (see Chapter 10). Be sure to stop and smell the roses, as it will make golf a much more rewarding and enjoyable experience.

In summary, make sure to acquire your golf equipment, take lessons whenever possible, and be sure to observe the etiquette associated with the game of golf. Abiding by the written and unwritten rules of golf will allow you and your fellow golfers to enjoy the journey all the more.

In closing, I want to wish you, the reader, much enjoyment and success with the game of golf and with the game of life itself. I truly hope you enjoyed and benefitted from this guide. Please feel free to e-mail me with any comments or questions at mikedeagle@optonline. net. Happy golfing *Fore Ever!*

Frustrated with your game? Tired of being confused about how to learn to play golf? *Golf Fore Ever* provides valuable information to the novice or newcomer to the sport to guide you through every step of the way. From purchasing your first set of golf clubs to scheduling your first time to play golf on a regulation course, this guide has all the information the beginning golfer needs to start to play. The information included between the pages of this book is derived from the author's thirty-plus years of personal experience playing this incredible sport. Reading this guide will make golf an even more enjoyable and rewarding experience for you and help you avoid the pitfalls encountered when first learning to play.

Golf Fore Ever will provide you with the necessary information to help you start to play golf the right way. The book tells you how and where to get proper instruction, cure the dreaded slice, and learn golf etiquette, an important but often-overlooked fundamental of the game. Along your journey learning to play golf, you will discover the delights and frustrations associated with the game. Golf can be a roller-coaster ride of emotions, from euphoria when you hit a career shot to a tight pin placement, to complete dismay when your ball finds the water or goes out of bounds on the very next hole. It is up to you to determine whether you will enjoy the ride and not let the game get the better of you. This guide will truly help you on your journey into the wonderful world of golf, for it is well worth the price of the ticket!